TO HELL AND BACK
WITH
CATATONIA

Brian Wright

TO HELL AND BACK
WITH
CATATONIA

'The Romance of Catatonia'
by
Brian Wright

FIRE
FLY
PUBLISHING

PUBLISHING

First published in 2001 by Firefly Publishing.
Firefly is an imprint of SAF Publishing Ltd in association
with Helter Skelter Publishing Ltd.

SAF Publishing
Unit 7, Shaftesbury Centre, 85 Barlby Road, London. W10 6BN
ENGLAND

www.safpublishing.com
www.skelter.demon.co.uk

ISBN 0 946719 36 5

All photographs © David Hardacre
Front cover photograph: Cerys Matthews at the Home International
concerts, Margam Park, South Wales, May 29, 1999

All lyrics quoted are for review, study or critical purposes.

A CIP catalogue record for this book is available from the British Library.

Printed in England by The Cromwell Press, Trowbridge, Wiltshire.

DEDICATION

This book is dedicated to the memory of Barry Cawley, Guitar Technician, and more importantly, a close friend of Catatonia, who was tragically killed on July 30th, 2000.

He will also be missed by Catatonia fans the world over.

> The stage is empty,
> Slowly, the fans move into place.
> Eyes focus expectantly forwards.
> A lone figure appears to tune and check guitars.
> His skilled hands and expert ears at work,
> On many a stage, in many a town,
> We all viewed him as our friend.
> But now the stage is empty,
> And sorrow is our song.

INTRODUCTION

People look at Catatonia and think it's me all the time. That it's me doing the lyrics and none of the music, and it's never been that simple, ever. Only the people who know us, know the score.

Cerys Matthews

My name is Brian and I am a Cataholic.

That is how some people view me. It is not an assessment that I would necessarily endorse, but there are very good reasons as to why I like the music of Catatonia. Indeed, I owe a hell of a lot to them. This book attempts to present a history of the group, and the part that their music played in rescuing me from the biggest personal crisis I have faced in my life.

I come from a very musical family. Most members either played instruments or sang. Amazingly, they were all self-taught. Whether this was because we were naturally gifted, or just tight-fisted Yorkshire folk who were too stingy to pay for lessons, is difficult to say. My parents did not buy a television until 1964, so I was brought up on a diet of listening to music on the radio (generally Radio Luxembourg), or playing my guitar in the bedroom. This tradition was further extended when my son David went on to eclipse all my guitar playing efforts.

As I grew older, I played in rock bands and sang as a solo folk singer for a good few years. When I quit singing I kept my hand in by helping at venues, and working with, or managing, new bands, generally on a part-time basis.

Then, in the early 1990s, I encountered personal tragedy. I lost my second wife, my mother and, against all odds, I survived a sub-arachnoid brain haemorrhage.

I soon plunged into a severe state of depression. As medication failed to offer any relief, I tried to end my life by serious alcohol abuse. I plummeted to depths I never knew existed. Every day was detested. I seemed to be in the deepest black pit on earth. I could not summon up the courage to do the final deed, so I chose to hit the bottle – big style. I would die of drink for sure, or I would kill myself whilst under the influence – an easy way out that had worked for many others. That was my plan. That was the ultimate objective.

Without my passionate love of music, I would not be alive. My self-destruction programme was all going to plan until I heard an unsigned band playing in Cardiff. It is ironic, in view of their reputation, that it should be Catatonia who saved me from drinking myself to death, but after following them for so long, you learn to expect the unexpected.

It might be dismissive to say they did not sound remarkable, yet there was something in their music, albeit then in a raw state, that grabbed my attention. I could not see them from where I stood, nor would it have been possible to focus on them through the drunken haze that surrounded my world. Yet something mystical reached out to me. I had found Catatonia, when I had lost everything else.

Drink had almost permanently put the angel on my shoulder to sleep, but through their music, Catatonia had begun to help me in my long battle against depression and an excessive consumption of alcohol. It was never plain sailing – often it was two steps forwards three steps back. In fact, in many ways, it resembled the career of the group.

From that fateful night I was to follow the band all over the place. At a time in my life when friends were justifiably in short supply, the band's songs replaced them. There were a number of occasions when their lyrics helped me cope with my problems and overcome my depression. Gradually, as I was able to pick up the pieces of my life, I discovered that there were lots of good bands in Wales, and I began a love affair with the country and its people that continues to this day.

This account then, is about music as a positive force. It is a side of pop music that often gets little coverage in the media. Bands do not set out with the intention of saving lives; they don't aspire to the role of social worker, but occasionally that is one of the end results of their efforts.

Finally, perhaps because of the problems that I had encountered during depression and nervous breakdown, I was very sensitive to the situation that Cerys found herself in during 1999 and 2000. If she can gain anything positive from this account, then I will have repaid some of the debt I feel I owe to the group.

* * *

Catatonia are a very private group of individuals and in chronicling their progress I have been very conscious of the need to respect their privacy. From early chats it was obvious that they were extremely sceptical of a book being written about them, and I promised that if ever they asked me not to publish, then I would honour that request.

As I progressed, I made sure a working draft was always available to band members and when the book was completed they said they had no objection. Nevertheless this is not an authorised biography. I had hoped to cover each member of the band equally. However, such is the presence of Cerys Matthews that I have been unable to achieve that objective, though I have tried to include as much information about the boys in the band as I could.

Individually and collectively, Catatonia have a varied and wicked sense of humour, something which we have in common, so I have tried to reflect this throughout the book. A book about Catatonia without humour would be like the Welsh flag without a dragon.

Because some of the book is about me, and the rest is about Catatonia, I had to ask myself a simple question, "Why was I attempting this book?"

The answer is that it is my thank you to the band, and my way of trying to give their fans the information that they have been seeking.

The history of Catatonia proves that if you have genuine talent and self-belief, then no matter how many times you shoot yourself in the foot, you can still walk on water.

I seek to make no money on the back of Catatonia. All I desire is to cover my costs. Any other revenue generated by sales of the book is to be given to charity(ies) nominated by the group.

After talking to some members of the band and their acquaintances, on an informal basis it was made clear to me that any such revenue should go to helping a charity concerned with cancer, to honour the memory of my late wife. I think you will appreciate where the decision came from, and I personally would like to thank the decision-makers. The charity I have chosen is PACT which is a Sheffield-based organisation devoted to the care and treatment of children diagnosed with cancer or leukaemia.

Finally I extend my gratitude to Aled, Cerys, Clancy, Dafydd, Mark, Owen and Paul. Thanks are also due to Debbie Prowse at *Welsh Bands Weekly* for all her faith in me, and the reassurances that she gave, and to Adam Shutes, Laura Derbyshire, Margot Saint, and all other Catatonia fans who helped me over the final stages with unstinting support.

THE VOICE

Cerys gets all the fame, we get well paid and fed well and so it's alright.
Mark Roberts

I actually know men who've fallen in love with Cerys after hearing her voice just once. Men who've never even seen her, who don't have the foggiest what she looks like, yet fall hopefully in love with her. Such is the power of her voice.
Welsh Bands Weekly

According to *The Concise Oxford Dictionary*, catatonia is "schizophrenia with intervals of catalepsy and occasional violence". This definition does not equate with the band either as individuals or as a group, although there are times when audiences are subjected to bouts of musical and vocal violence interspersed with strains of tenderness.

Catatonia's media coverage has focussed predominantly on the singer, often quite unfairly at the expense of the other musicians, mainly because of the unique vocal range of Cerys Matthews. "The Voice" is not an unknown epithet bestowed on vocalists. The music press started allocating this accolade to Cerys Matthews in 1996, around the time of *Way Beyond Blue*. As the career of the band developed, so the vocal range and quality of their singer attracted a wide range of descriptions from an appreciative and imaginative press.

The *New Musical Express* described her as sounding like, "Shirley Bassey putting five pints of Jack Daniels (with snakebite chasers) into the Grand

Canyon through a megaphone during an earthquake", while *The Times* eulogised "a gorgeous Welsh lilt that sounds as intricate and warming as a crocheted blanket".

"Blessed with a voice of such emotional range, that she can sound breathy, hormonal, lurid and seductive in the time it takes Celine Dion to draw a breath," was *The Independent on Sunday's* view.

To this day, Cerys still maintains that her voice is no different to that of her sister. After Catatonia had established themselves with the album *International Velvet*, she modestly stated, "I've never really rated my voice. I thought it was the same as anybody else's. It just seems to have got stronger over the years. I get all these people saying it's brilliant and I find that quite strange. I sing all the time, that's my main hobby."

Clearly the press continued to think that it was anything but an ordinary voice. To *Melody Maker* it, "hinted at forbidden pleasures: breathless, sharpened, familiar yet utterly beguiling. Simultaneously – sweet and corrupting. Staggering, desolate." *Sky* magazine more bluntly felt, "it would strip paint off the walls of any scabby venue". Perhaps the key to it all is summed up when she says, "When I'm singing, I'm no longer Cerys, it's part of a dream." However not everyone was captivated. Neil Hannon from the Divine Comedy much less flatteringly commented, "Cerys sounds like she's laying eggs."

Initially, the media compared Cerys to Bjork. However, before long, critics were praising her for one of the most distinctive voices in music. She has also been tagged with having one of the sexiest voices in pop, a raunchy style not heard since Janis Joplin.

Cerys' speaking voice is even sexier, made more so by her love of phrases that could be considered quaint and old fashioned. Her nationality helps. Two expressive things about her voice are traits of the Welsh language; open vowels and the rolling "R". Significantly, she appreciates one of Julio Iglesias' selling points is mispronouncing English. Cerys is quietly spoken, but punctuates her conversation with smiles that are guaranteed to make you feel at ease.

Having a distinctive voice is no guarantee of success, however. Ann Matthews, who sang with Welsh bands Y Fflapp and Ectogram throughout the nineties possesses a similar vocal talent, but few people outside of Wales have ever heard of her. There are other factors that need to be in place before any vocalist can achieve fame. Raw ambition and a determination to succeed are key elements.

However, contrary to the views of many media commentators, Catatonia is not simply Cerys and Co – a singer plus four journeymen hired hands. Cerys is the first to acknowledge this. "It pisses me off when they go on about my voice – there's more going on with us. Sometimes people write about us and ignore the boys completely, when in fact we're a full band where everybody contributes."

Certainly, when Catatonia formed, the voice of Cerys had yet to mature and develop the vocal prowess it possesses today. She would, and will, always sing, any time, any place, given the chance. But she had to be given the chance. "The Voice" had to make a journey to get to its public. This is the route it took.

YOU'VE GOT A LOT TO ANSWER FOR

MARK ROBERTS
Guitarist, backing vocals & songwriter

We haven't done anything interesting enough to justify a book.
Mark Roberts speaking to the author in June 1999

Mark was born in the town of Llanrwst in Gwynedd, North Wales on November 3rd 1969, making him the youngest member of the group. He is a distant relative of the fifties pop star and entertainer Tommy Steele.

Mark first thought about being in a band at school. "It was when I was about eleven. I think it was just seeing bands, but not one particular moment. People used to bring records into school, New Wave-type singles at the time."

Mark chose the guitar as his instrument, but initially struggled to get the hang of it. He temporarily switched to drums and took lessons at school. This had the added bonus of enabling him to miss French classes.

Soon he was hooked on pop music and started going to gigs. "I remember seeing Dexy's Midnight Runners in Llandudno as a kid and it was fucking brilliant just to see a big band."

Behind the bluster of publicity that always surrounds Cerys, many forget that Mark has developed into one of the best songwriters in the British music scene, seldom getting the recognition he deserves. When people suggest Cerys should go solo because of her exceptional vocals, it is easy to lose sight of the fact that every singer needs a song, and without Mark Roberts to provide them, Catatonia would never have existed. Even though he admits to being motivated by money, Mark possesses a talent that money simply cannot buy.

"My teachers would say, 'Why haven't you done your homework?'" he comments. "And I would say, 'Oh, I've been writing songs,' and I would be sent to the Head. A year later when I was on Welsh TV, they'd come up and apologise."

Mark was about 15 or 16 when he embarked on his first serious venture in pop music, founding Y Cyrff (The Bodies), a Welsh language rock band, along with future Catatonia bass player, Paul Jones. They recorded videos for the Welsh TV pop programme *Roc Ar Ol Te* (Rock For Tea), which earned them enough money for a couple of low-key singles. Y Cyrff went on to release two albums on the Ankst label, *Llawenydd Heb Ddiwedd* (Endless Joy) and *Mae Ddoe Yn Ddoe* (Yesterday Is Yesterday), along with a single "Hwyl Fawr Heulwen" (Goodbye Sunshine). Mark, Paul, and fellow band members Barry Cawley (guitar) and Mark Kendall (drums), performed with such total irreverence that the local music press tagged them "the rebel band."

Owen Powell of Catatonia rated Y Cyrff as "the biggest thing in Wales for a while after The Alarm." To me, Y Cyrff seemed to be The Clash 'Cymru-style' with a chainsaw massacre drive to their music. Mark was on vocals and always seemed to be changing either the style or the colour of his hair. This did not appear to be wasted on one of their fans, a certain Ms Matthews, who several years later, would continue this trend. He also often sung with his eyes closed and was wary of crowds in confined spaces.

Y Cyrff disbanded in 1991 without providing Mark with the wealth he craved. He made ends meet with spells as a butcher, potato picker, electrician's mate and working for a pet food firm called Pero.

Mark's favourite bands include The Clash and The Alarm, although the Boomtown Rats were his first love. He sometimes plays Clash songs at soundchecks and takes in Joe Strummer gigs whenever possible. Quirkily true to the spirit of punk, when shopping for records he only buys singles.

Mark has always been a keen footballer, and even now loves spending some of his off-duty hours playing five-a-side, but concedes that now he plays well back and lets the others do the running.

Like Cerys, he supports Manchester United. It may seem strange for a devout Welshman to follow a team from Manchester, but he became a United fan because a bus going to Old Trafford used to pass where he lived, and he claims it was a better option than watching Wrexham. I am proud to say that my team, Sheffield Wednesday, has a 100% record against Man Utd at Wembley.

PAUL JONES
Bass, occasional songwriter

We prefer to work out of Wales if we can. Paul Jones

Paul hails from Llanrwst. Born on February 5th 1960, he is the senior member of the band. Prior to his career in music he worked for the National Trust as an instructor in dry stone walling techniques.

During Paul's fondly remembered Y Cyrff days he sported a quiff hair-style and played the bass in frenetic fashion, similar to Norman Watt-Roy of the Blockheads. Now his technique is more in the laidback tradition of Bill Wyman of the Rolling Stones.

He explains that in his early career, "I used to put too much effort into playing bass, probably as I've got small hands – they get cramped up. I was holding my shoulders really badly and I used to get swellings in my lower arms. I suppose that was stage fright really."

He was into bands from an early age and his music tastes vary from rap acts Ice-T and NWA to the Beatles and the Stones. His love of Jacques Brel shows its influence in some of the band's songs such as "No Stone Unturned".

Generally found at the back of the stage near Aled's drum kit, Paul sees Cerys' occasional solo acoustic number as a welcome opportunity to sit down and smoke a cigarette. He claims that if he occasionally feels the need for attention, "I just stop playing and everybody gasps."

Paul is the proud father of a young daughter Gwen. I will not mention Paul's partner's name, because the first few times I met her I could never remember it. This led to her refusing to tell me her name in case I put in this book.

ALED RICHARDS
Drums , occasional songwriter

No, it wasn't fucking me that sang 'The Snowman'. Aled Richards

Born in Llanelli in West Wales on July 5th 1969, Aled's early memories include banging on an array of pots and pans in time to *Top of the Pops*. Aged fourteen and several sets of kitchen utensils later, he was playing drums in Beatles covers bands, the members of which were many years his senior. He became interested in progressive rock and played in the youthful rock group It's a Go. He joined Catatonia following the departure of drummer Daf Ieuan to the Super Furry Animals.

If ever you're in a record shop, and there is a guy with long hair, putting copies of Catatonia's CDs to the front of the shelves before buying one himself, the odds are it will be Aled. He is especially proud of his one-and-a-half-hour mini disc compilation of the band's B-sides.

Aled still lives in Llanelli with his two children. He enjoys reading poetry and like Cerys is a competent keyboard player. According to Owen, "Aled is a very good pianist, but not when anyone else is in the room. So you have to leave the room and hide behind the door, and then he starts playing these beautiful, classical pieces, but as soon as you walk back in, he won't do it."

One of his cousins is a certain Mr David Evans of Aberystwyth, aka U2's The Edge.

OWEN POWELL
Guitarist, songwriter

We've all done other jobs, most of which we didn't enjoy. Maybe you appreciate your success more if it happens when you're older. Owen Powell

Owen was born on July 9th 1967, in Cambridge. His brother was also born in England in Lancaster, but both were raised in South Wales by authentically Welsh parents. His middle names are Charles Morgan which were his great-grandfather's names. Like Mark, his peers were also proved to be hopeless prophets, "My teachers said, 'You'll never earn money making music.'"

Owen is eternally good-natured and very philosophical as befits a keen reader. Indeed, one of his previous jobs required him to wheel round a hospital reading trolley. His optimistic nature might have to do with him being a fan of Cardiff City more than anything else. As well as his guitar playing, Owen's talents extend to being able to play "a bit of drums".

In addition to music and football, one of his interests is boxing, largely because his father was a devotee of the sport. As a treat, he was allowed to stay up and watch title fights. One of his heroes was Marvin Hagler, who Owen rated as "the coolest person on earth". Owen also has the distinction of being the first member of Catatonia to appear on television when he briefly appeared as a cheeky schoolboy in the S4C soap *Pobol Y Cym* in 1977.

It was music however that was to take up most of his time. One of Owen's earliest musical influences was a Welsh band called Datblygu who were fronted by actor David R Edwards. They achieved a little recognition outside of Wales being played by veteran BBC DJ John Peel, as well as appearing on *The Tube*.

Owen began going to watch bands at the age of twelve, and as he grew older a lot of his summers were spent at rock festivals. The first major one he attended was at Reading "sometime in the eighties", when one of the featured groups was The Stranglers. During the afternoon Owen and

his friends woke up with horrible sunburn after falling asleep having consumed three plastic litre bottles they had filled with cheap British sherry.

A useful festival ploy was to wear a bottle-opener around his neck. "I
went to Glastonbury with one of them tied with a piece of string. I met
more people than you'd ever believe possible. Plus it's a fantastic way of
getting free beer."

As a punter Owen used to think that all the bands stayed for the whole
time, hanging out together, but experience has taught him that it is not
like that at all. "You arrive a couple of hours beforehand and just bugger
off straight after. You're flung on this stage with no soundcheck or anything, then there's this amazing adrenaline rush."

Periods of being on the dole, interspersed with being a member of the
underground Welsh band The Crumblowers, and then subsequently a
spell with the group U Thant, were to be Owen's lot for the late eighties
and early nineties.

To pass time, he took drum lessons at the Grass Roots Studio in Cardiff for only £1 an hour, where he met other musicians. Originally a bass
player, he progressed to guitar technician with Catatonia before becoming
the last member to join the band. This crucial move allowed "The Voice"
to put down her guitar and concentrate mainly on singing.

CERYS MATTHEWS
Vocalist, songwriter

1969 was a remarkable year in many ways. It marked the end of the "Swing-ing Sixties", and man in the form of Neil Armstrong first set foot on the moon. It was also the year of the Woodstock festival and Charles Windsor being invested as the Prince of Wales.

In the USA, America's daughters were swooning over "weeds with beards", whilst their mothers were starting what has now become a regular showbiz tradition. During a tour following a highly successful TV special *This is Tom Jones '69*, these ladies threw their knickers on stage as Tiger Tom drove them wild.

On the subject of music and Wales, another significant event in Welsh cultural history took place in 1969. In St David's Hospital in Cardiff, on Friday, April 11th, a baby girl was born to the Matthews family. Their second child, and their second daughter, they were to have two more chil-dren, both boys.

In 1999, Cerys was to comment that, "My mother got this advice from my grandmother on contraception when she married. 'You can take the train to London but you can always get off at Reading.' But it didn't work. She didn't want to get off... We're a big family, very close."

Over the next few months, this baby would squawk and wail like other babies, but the infant was giving her family the first demo of what was to become known as "The Voice".

When I originally asked someone what the names of the group were, the person was kind enough to write them down for me, even though at that time I seemed to be seeing everything double. I could not pronounce "Cerys", I had never come across the name before and assumed it was a squiggle on the piece of paper, so that is how I came to refer to her as "The Lady". By the time I had mastered the linguistic problem, Cerys was tell-ing everyone "I'm a laydee", so who was I to argue?

Cerys' middle names are Elizabeth Philip, her mother apparently chose Philip because it is Cerys' father's name. I haven't seen the birth certificate

so have no way of checking this information, but Cerys does have a reputation for taking the piss, so who knows.

Her father, Philip Matthews, was a Doctor in Orthopaedics, working
at amongst other places, Morriston Hospital, whilst her mother, Pauline,
undertook the hardest job of all, bringing up four children, before going
into teaching.

Cerys' early childhood memories include nightmares about being stran-
gled in the vast array of plant life that she kept in her bedroom, plus her
favourite childhood pastime of eating worms in the garden and bugs in
the fields. She had more than a passing interest in plants and animals at
that age. She recalls having a huge tantrum when she was four years old,
because the hamsters were stuck in cages in Cardiff market. Other early
loves in her life were animals of a less fluffy or real variety. Her plastic
Dougal dog, Pinky and Perky, The Wombles (her all-time heroes), Lassie
the dog, and Pippi Longstocking, were all childhood favourites.

At that same age, she demonstrated her independence and ingenuity by
removing the stabilisers from her bicycle. Even though she kept falling
off, she learned to ride it, and considered this to be "probably my greatest
achievement". Also, as a six-year-old – a precursor of pavement rage – she
was given a pair of old metal roller skates as a Christmas present. Precari-
ous verging on the dangerous, she spent hours and hours on them she
loved them so much.

As an indication of what the future held in store, a very young Cerys
had her first starring role. At the house where she lived there was a massive
stone in the back of the garden. It was big enough for a child to lie on, and
it was shaped like a stone sun-bed. "It made me feel like Cleopatra," but
not for very long as, "my parents hired a JCB and pushed it into the stream
at the bottom of our garden and spoilt all my fun."

Perhaps as a result of the traumas of his work as a surgeon, her father
raised his children very much without kid gloves.

Aged eleven, Cerys fractured her arm. "It was completely bent out of
shape, and all my parents did was laugh! 'Oh! That's a funny shape isn't it
darling! Now have an aspirin and go to bed, you're annoying us!'"

But there was also a lot of care and love in the Matthews' household,
and it was against this background that her personality and sense of values
developed. She grew up to like receiving attention, but more important
was her enjoyment in returning the compliment with interest to those she
was close to.

Testing the boundaries, just to see how far it is possible to go, is a part of most people's formative years. "I was probably kicked up the butt a fair few times. It's given me a good healthy obsession with fighting," Cerys recalls. "I always used to take the opposite course to whatever my parents, my family, my schooling told me," is her take on how early parental discipline affected her.

Clearly the self-belief, the independence, the disarming mischievous streak were all blossoming in her at an early age. Content with the knowledge and security that she had a good and loving family, Cerys put all her energy into being a nuisance.

As a child, she remembers always being scolded for misbehaving, her parents thinking she was prone to fits, "because I'd throw so many tantrums when I didn't get my own way, I'd go blue in the face and they'd think I was dead." On a number of occasions they would take her to hospital and discover that there was nothing wrong with her. It was just pure temper.

Cerys' father appears to be a loveable eccentric. For example, he would put dead rabbits and chicken legs in the family freezer to carry out medical experiments in his spare time. This was not wasted on his curious daughter, who would take the chicken legs to school to show off to her friends.

There were also artificial hips around the house and a real skeleton called Charlie that the children would play with. They would put him in various positions and make him smoke a pipe.

Whether or not it was as a result of growing up amidst these domestic trappings, the young Cerys became very philosophical. "Right from when I was ten, I realised you could live your life by logic, but I have a massive vacuum to be filled by passion and romance."

She had already begun wondering about what the future had in store.

"I had a friend who was a girl, and she used to try and kip in my bed all the time. We weren't lesbians or anything – she just used to share my bed with me – and talk all night long, going, 'You're special, and I'm special' and I never believed her. I thought it was bollocks. I wanted to do something 'special'. I think special is better than famous. The point is, I wanted to do something unpredictable – out of the ordinary. But I'd like to meet up with her now."

At her primary school, Cerys earned the nickname "the dentist", due to her helpful habit of removing the loosening milk teeth of her fellow classmates. It was here that she had her first experimental snog (possibly also in the name of dental research). "I was nine, in primary school and we were taken to a lot of field centres to learn about plants. So, we could run wild in the country," Cerys remembers. "And it's a natural thing to do, isn't it. Experiment."

The same year, she also managed to acquire a discoloured and broken front tooth of her own, when she head-butted a boy at school and her tooth became embedded in his forehead.

As a result of Mr Matthews occupation, the family were used to relocating houses regularly and when Cerys was about seven they left Cardiff, necessitating a change of schools.

On reaching secondary school her mind was made up that the classroom and abject boredom went hand in hand. There was more to life than this: such as booze, boys, truancy, smoking and platform soles. Her ideas of what was suitable school attire led to regular visits to the Headmaster for contravening the dress code.

The routine schedule of prescribed schoolwork was supplemented with more interesting activities. Dissecting rats in biology was enlivened by seeing how quickly a Bunsen burner could destroy a biro. Anyone who had left their bag open was prey to a competition to see who could spit the furthest into it, with guess who, being a regular winner. In addition to the chicken's legs, on one occasion she also took a human index finger into school. Presumably to cock a digit at authority.

As the supply of milk teeth declined and the Tooth Fairy in Cardiff and Swansea filed for bankruptcy, Cerys' "the dentist" tag was replaced by the nickname "Squeaky". "Because I had a really high voice and when I used to get frustrated or excited, it would become... squeaky."

Cerys was an intelligent and extremely confident young girl, giving her peers the impression that she would succeed in whatever career she chose to follow. Initially she attempted to sing in the school choir, though performing religious laments was not something she enjoyed, and her voice failed to register any significant attention. She did excel in languages, but often schoolwork proved too easy for her and this led to frequent daydreaming and thinking about boys. In the confines of the classroom an active mind also made her angry with life and fuelled rebellious behaviour.

Her response was to bunk off for teenage drinking sessions down the local shopping centre or park, a more enjoyable alternative to lessons. Alcohol, music and Cerys became close friends at quite an early age. She began forcing whisky down her throat when she was about ten or eleven because Bob Dylan used to drink it, but now claims, "To be absolutely honest, I always hated the taste of it!" She also discovered the pleasures of smoking, with the added attraction that it gave her voice a gruff, sexy quality.

She certainly learned the ABC at an early age – alcohol, boys and cigarettes. Boys were never far from her thoughts, and because of her love of animals, the outdoor life and working with her hands, her ambition was to marry a farmer.

Cerys claims that in her teens she, "always wanted to be a boy, because they were allowed to play football and to do woodwork, while all the girls had to go to life classes where teachers prepare you for all the horrors of becoming a lady."

There were some activities though, that appealed to the adolescent Cerys. Cross-country running, for instance, was enjoyable because it gave her the chance to have a fag without the teachers being around. She also became pretty good at hockey, but was more renowned for her off-the-ball action. With sports, it was not the actual taking part bit, but the adrenaline buzz afterwards. She also tried her hand at rugby and broke somebody's leg. "I'm not proud of that," she confesses, "but it happens."

As I have followed Catatonia, I have become amazed at the number of people who claim to have been in the same class at school as Cerys. Admittedly she went to quite a few schools, but as these people's ages range from 24 to 45, at least some of their claims must be spurious. I know for a fact, that a couple of the blokes went to all-boys schools – although it doesn't appear that an all-boys school would have been too much of a hardship for this particular young lady.

There are two former pupils whose memories appear to be more reliable. Firstly, Kirsty Williams, the Welsh Assembly member for Brecon and Radnorshire, says she will always remember the way Cerys saved her from the school bullies at St Michael's private school in Llanelli.

"She was a year older than me and was always getting into trouble for the way she dressed and so on. She was pretty fearless even then and stood no nonsense. If she wanted to borrow your Walkman you didn't argue, you just handed it over. But she was always very fair, and always stuck up for the underdog. If someone was being bullied she would sort it out. I was being picked on once by a group of people and Cerys just stepped in and put a stop to it, she told them to cut it out and they certainly listened. She was a good person to have around, especially when you're the youngest in your class."

Paul Morgan also has memories of St Michael's:

"Cerys and I both went to an independent school and it took us about fifty minutes to get there on the school bus. She lived maybe the furthest from the school, so on the way home it was just me, Cerys and a few others. I never saw her get in trouble, I think she was quite calm in school. She was quite a bit younger than me but clearly quite pretty, though my eyes didn't stray that far. And she lived in quite a big house – I always used to look in.

"She was one of the thirteen-year olds, that the older teenagers took an interest in, because she was so mature. She was at ease talking to all ages, she hasn't changed that much actually. She never seemed to do anything musical at school – it was a very rural school – there was only one shop nearby and that was it. There weren't any opportunities for bands to play.

"It was pretty hard to miss her, to be honest, yet until this Christmas (1998), I had no idea that Cerys in Catatonia was the same little Cerys I knew on the bus. It was quite a shock, but I thought about it and it all made sense – even at the age of thirteen, she was vivacious in character and I always remember her having beads in her hair. The beads thing is interesting, because being at an independent school, having quite a strict uniform, it was difficult to be rebellious, but she did her best."

At school's out forever time, Cerys finished up with "A" grades in typing and needlework, and an "E" in biology. It was never confirmed whether she graduated with honours in boys, booze and baccy, or if she beat the Welsh truancy record.

Cerys sums up her adolescent years by saying, "I was a bit of an obnoxious bitch as a teenager. I was always the first to try anything."

Certainly, she tried a number of different images in her adolescent years. She went through a goth phase, a punk phase, and at one time was well into 2-Tone. "I had the complete uniform – pork pie hat, Sta-prest trousers, and skinny tie – but unfortunately I didn't have any records. That wasn't a total success," she recalls.

Being an attractive teenager with a lust for life, she soon found that youthful pleasures can cause parental concern. "The usual shenanigans you know. It wasn't that terrible," Cerys remembers. "Take the three heavenly sins, mix them together, and have a charity walk for the local chapel. Pass by Swansea Leisure Centre with your mother and all her friends, and um, well, they caught me at it." The occasion caused her pocket money, and that of her three siblings to be stopped.

Her education in music developed in her bedroom, much the same as mine did, although separated by a generation and 200 miles. She picked up the acoustic guitar in her early teens and began learning amongst other things a combination of Beatles, Hank Williams, Smokey Robinson and ancient Welsh folk songs.

Nobody really knew about her guitar playing and songwriting until she was about twenty, except for her brothers who were briskly admonished for invading her space when she was playing. These sessions would be committed to tape in the way other people keep diaries.

For relaxation, her family listened to a lot of old-fashioned songs from black and white movies, like those starring Frank Sinatra or Doris Day, and also Welsh folk music and Ivor Novello. These are songs that are still popular with Cerys today. However, her singing inspiration came largely through participation, rather than any particular artist or recording. This did not become apparent to her until later in her career, when a good friend reminded her, "You always said in interviews that you have no musical background at all. Bollocks! You lot never shut up."

After a little thought, Cerys realised that the observation was correct. In fact, singing ran in the family, certainly amongst the females. Her mother regularly listened and sang along to Radio 2 whilst doing the housework, and one of her aunts who used to visit regularly would sing to anyone who'd listen.

In addition to the music that the family enjoyed, Cerys was developing her own eclectic tastes in music. She liked Toyah Wilcox (and dyed her hair accordingly). Artists as diverse as Billie Holliday, Bob Dylan, David Bowie, Smokey Robinson, The Doors, Abba, The Hollies, Leo Sayer and Scott Walker were also among her many favourites.

During her early teens when she used to go to see local bands, she would always watch the lads getting into a transit with all their gear; her one ambition was to be sat in the front of the van and driving off and going places. It was not primarily that she wanted to be out there singing, it was a mixture of wanderlust and curiosity. In fact, "I never admitted to wanting to be a pop star," she says.

Her first real crush was on David Soul, which was encouraged by her sister regularly playing "Don't Give Up On Us Baby" and "Silver Lady" at home. It was also her New Romantic sister who took Cerys to her first proper gig in 1984, when they went to see Wham at The Roxy in Swansea.

Cerys was persuaded to attend by being told that "nobody this big would ever come to Swansea again" and that she would regret it forever if she missed out, because "this was bigger than Elvis".

Although convinced by her sister's sales pitch, Cerys remembers thinking that George Michael had a lot of eating to do to be bigger than Elvis.

At the gig, she was far from impressed with the antics of George Michael and Andrew Ridgeley playing shuttlecock games on stage, and rather than look at their gyrations she focussed her eyes on something she had not seen before – a mixing desk. However, It wasn't long before she attended a gig by someone that she did like – Billy Bragg – and she was hooked.

Holidays, outings, and Christmas times are special to most families and the Matthews family was no exception. Except – they did it their way.

On one of her early childhood outings in the Matthews family car, a trailer that was trundling along in front of them lost one of its passengers – a huge sow. The pig came flying out of the trailer and was almost knocked over by the Matthewsmobile. The farmer got out and chased it. The family choir, seated in their car, started singing an old Welsh folk song about the days when each household would keep a pig as a family pet, until the sad time came to eat it. Unfortunately, this particular sow was run over before the farmer could get to it.

Like all caring parents, Mr Matthews tried to ensure his offspring were entertained when vacation time arrived. But Cerys, for one, was not totally impressed by these offerings.

"The stereo system in our house was so bad, I didn't know what treble sounded like until I was at least twenty-one," she explains. But that did not stop her father from compiling music tapes, which he called "Pops". "We had to listen to these dreadful tapes… We'd end up hearing them about a million times because he would only bring three away in case he lost any," she recalls.

Another of her father's rather eccentric ideas was to put foil inside the car windows to keep them cool. This had the opposite effect and prevented the enjoyment of travel games such as car spotting. Other forms of entertainment had to be found. So, "I just spent my time picking chicken pox off my brother's chin", she remembers.

Some childhood summers were spent in Pembrokeshire, a place still much loved by the family, so much so that her parents have now retired there. Her father now mills flour and builds fake megalithic stoneworks (Cromlechs). Much amusement can be gained from watching tourists taking pictures of these, but as Cerys points out that they also have a more practical application, that of "providing something for the cows to scratch their arses on."

"Pembrokeshire feels like the end of the world – but in a nice way…",
she continues. "I always know that if I can go for a long walk on the cliffs,
then everything will be OK."

Christmas Day is remembered for just such walks. "Dad said things like,
'Anyone fancy a walk?'" she says. "You know what that is. It's 'cos folks
have eaten too much and they want to fart. All the kids are moaning,
going, 'What are we doing?' and all the adults are striding ahead going
'Smell that fresh air'. Except they're farting away. And you're in the wake
going, 'Call that fresh?' There's no fresh air for children at Christmas."

Having managed to survive these annual poison gas attacks, she remembers one of the best Christmases as being the time when she was seventeen
and her dad got annihilated on home brew. "Seven of the men were so ill
that night that they ran out of buckets!", she recalls. Cerys herself was too
excited at listening to everybody singing Christmas songs and watching
Judy Garland on TV to get that drunk.

Nowadays, the Matthews family Christmas still carries on, and their
famous daughter still loves to be at home for the festivities.

"It's a Christmas tradition for me to fall out with my mum over the cooking. It depends on who wins the argument, who stays in the kitchen, and
who storms out in disgust. It's her house, which gives her a bit of an advantage, but I've got youth on my side."

With her schooldays behind her, Cerys set about life in the great wide
world. There followed a succession of jobs interspersed with times on the
dole. One particular job, working behind a local bar in Pembrokeshire,
would stand her in good stead in later years. It was here during singing
sessions held after hours that she was first told that she was a good singer.

"There was this guy from America who told me that I sounded like
the seventies singer Melanie and that I should do some recording," she
proudly states.

Many of the jobs taught Cerys about the realities of life the hard way.
The worst job was cleaning saucepans in a restaurant. Having been told
she was going to be a waitress, she donned her best clothes, only to find
on arrival that she was led directly to the kitchen where she was faced with
the sight of the biggest pans she'd ever seen. Her reward for cleaning these
was a princely £1.20p an hour. She stuck at it for just one night.

Like many kids, her seventeenth birthday coincided with her first driving lesson – only to result in her promptly driving straight into the back of
some unfortunate person's car. Undeterred she carried on, and passed her
driving test first time.

"Yes, but it was Christmas, and I'm sure the examiner was drunk after a work do," she remembers. "He kept trying to make jokes – on testing my Highway Code, he showed me the uneven road sign and just chuckled, saying 'It's just a bumpity road isn't it? Just a bumpity road.'"

Twelve years later, she would buy her first car – ironically from the proceeds of "Road Rage".

After turning eighteen Cerys moved to London to study psychiatric nursing at the Middlesex Hospital, but soon realised she was not up to the emotional rigours of the job. Despite her claim to be "fascinated by the recesses of the human mind" she quit the training after a year. Her decision to try nursing had been motivated by her family's medical background. The fact that her sister is a nurse, her aunt a radiographer, her uncle a GP, and her father a retired surgeon clearly influenced her decision of "attempting to keep everyone happy". But the National Health Service was never going to be Cerys' vocation in life.

In any event, this was not the same NHS that had been pioneered by one of her heroes, Aneurin Bevan. "It could be so brilliant," she bemoans. "But with the NHS becoming more Americanised, the standard of instruction is below par, and at the end of it was the prospect of becoming an underpaid nurse."

While searching to find her niche in life, she noticed an advert in the appropriately titled magazine – *The Lady* – for a nannying job in Barcelona, in the Catalan part of Spain. She accepted the position and by the end of the year had learnt to speak Spanish, becoming fluent in Catalan, to complement her excellent Welsh and basic French. Her love for languages is heightened by a fascination with how people use different ways to say things – particularly when it comes to swearwords.

In Barcelona, for respite, Cerys played folk songs on her acoustic guitar to amuse the children in her care, whilst they mischievously water-bombed her in return. Spain also indulged another of her great passions – cooking – and it was here that she "learnt how to cook a great tortilla."

However, the job also afforded lighter moments. One particular night she was invited to a fancy dress party. "I was dressed up as a mountain," she recalls. "It was awful though, nobody knew what I was supposed to be! I had my face painted green, and I had green hair and I had sheep stuck all around my thighs. Mountains don't come without sheep, do they? I liked my hair green though."

After achieving the dubious distinction of being the least identifiable mountain in Spain, she eventually returned to Cardiff. Once settled back on native soil, Cerys went to Fishguard High School to study French and Welsh at 'A' Level. She was unemployed, but possessing a natural tendency to get fidgety, it was necessary to keep her mind ticking over and active. So, back in Wales, Cerys' hedonistic tendencies were also back in full flow. It was very much a case of "lock up your sons" when her posse hit town. When she was pubbing and clubbing with her mates, if a man attracted her, she would take the lead, "cos actually, if I fancied a guy, I'd just go for it. They used to call me 'Jumping Jack Flash'."

Living life to excess can always have its downside, and Cerys made one of her many unsuccessful attempts to quit drinking when she started seeing pig's ears growing out of people's heads. As consolation to the brewing and distilling industries, these attempts to sign the pledge were only ever temporary.

On entering her twenties, Cerys commented, "My mum is just relieved I'm out of my teens. She's just like sitting on the edge of a motorway breathing a sigh of relief and thinking, 'Thank fuck that's over.'"

On leaving Fishguard High School, she found that jobs were hard to come by. The social fabric of industrial Britain had been devastated by Thatcherite policies, and many towns were now centres of high unemployment. Cerys claims that she was on-and-off the dole for about five years, and would not have survived without it. Eventually she found a far from glamorous day-job as a beach cleaner for the local council, picking up waste and dead seagulls washed up from the sea onto the beach. She admitted to becoming a specialist in removing the corpses of seals.

"I used to drive around all day with the radio on. Then I'd get to the beach and do a bit of cleaning up in my red bikini and those massive Council work gloves. I was Madame Cholet from the Wombles – swimsuit issue. I've always admired the Wombles and their philosophy of finding a use for everything."

The job was poorly paid, but she admitted, "I spent the entire time looking for drugs (didn't find any)". In the end she settled for some lovely shipwreck items which were to adorn her mantelpiece at home.

Up until this point Cerys' early years can best be summed up as a rare amalgam of Boadicea, Mrs Beaton and Jenny Lee, all wrapped up in the frame of the Matthews' youngest daughter. A genuine free spirit that challenged authority at every step, she was nonetheless determined to succeed, and to defend fair play. This was a time for developing her own sense of values.

People who possess an artistic temperament tend to have a very sensitive and vulnerable side to their nature, which they sometimes try to conceal by their up-front, over-the-top behaviour. And Cerys is no different. She is no fool, but readily plays down her intelligence and pokes fun at herself when it suits. But having always steadied herself with an enduring love of her family and friends, it has often provided her with a refuge when living in the fast lane.

SWEET, SWEET, SWEET, SWEET, CATATONIA

Boy sees, boy takes, boy hooked. Matthews/Roberts

So why "The Romance of Catatonia" subtitle? The first book that my father bought me was *The Romance of the Wednesday*, written by R. Sparling in the 1930s about the history of Sheffield Wednesday Football Club. It was set at a time when they used to win things; such as football matches.

In literature, a romance is a tale of love and adventure, remote from the concerns of everyday life – a sometime fantasy. Neither Catatonia, nor unfortunately Sheffield Wednesday, are fantasy and both are dear to my heart – but this book is about Catatonia.

Whether Catatonia are remote from everyday life depends on how you live your own. As for fantasy, if you had told a couple of young buskers in Cardiff in 1992 the heights that their group would achieve in 1998 and beyond, then...

The prospective players in this romance have already been depicted. Initially the stage that would become theirs was South Wales.

For over a decade and a half South Wales has seen an evolutionary process that has produced a vast array of bands covering virtually every musical style. It has become as prolific as areas such as Merseyside and typifies the musical culture of industrial Britain.

I have talked to many people who are active in the music business in Wales, and over the years I have tried to convince them that they are very fortunate in having this quantity of homegrown talent. By and large they tend to dismiss it, mainly on the mistaken assumption that every other area is similarly blessed. This is not the case.

Most of the bands are based in Swansea, Cardiff or Newport. But in general, bands from elsewhere in Wales tend to move to Cardiff if they are trying to improve their lot. Cardiff has always been a beautiful city. Old buildings have been renovated and a massive programme of development and refurbishment is transforming it into one of Europe's most progressive cities.

The nightlife is vibrant but there is a growing concern amongst those who love live music that many venues now host DJ sets at the expense of live bands. A lot of venues that do cater for live bands merely tend to book covers artists rather than those who play original material. Having successfully developed a generation of musicians and singers, it would be tragic if there were to be only limited opportunities available in the future. Cerys herself has pointed out that, apart from the University, few outlets for original bands now exist in Cardiff City centre.

The major exception to this is Clwb Ifor Bach, known popularly as The Welsh Club. Here the best selection of local/visiting/signed/unsigned bands can be seen several nights a week. At least one of these nights – Jon Wing's Xxplosure night – is largely dedicated to new bands. It has been an early stepping stone for Stereophonics, Supernaturals, 3 Colours Red, Arab Strap and Catatonia.

It is against this background that the romance of Catatonia began to unfold, starting their journey into the limelight, often progressing via the long scenic route.

In 1991 following the demise of Y Cyrff, Mark tried a handful of jobs while still continuing to studiously write songs, collecting them in "notebooks full of horrible lyrics." He had also begun a relationship with Cerys who had been an Y Cyrff groupie. As a result the couple moved into a house in Gold Street in Cardiff's Adamstown district.

Here they struggled to make ends meet, both were experiencing difficulties in securing worthwhile employment. As a way of bringing in extra income the pair decided to start busking. Cerys had always harboured a desire to break into the music industry; to write songs and to sing, and this was the lowest point of entry.

A publicity story put out in their early days stated that their origins stemmed from the moment when an onlooker – transfixed by Cerys singing "That's Entertainment" and a Spanish song "Llorona" – approached her. He told them that he liked her voice, but was not too keen on the music she was playing. Fortuitously, he also had a guitar string of the same gauge that she was missing from her acoustic guitar. The good Samaritan turned out to be Mark Roberts.

As the band progressed, the story followed them around. But however romantic it sounds, it was a complete concoction. The band's thinking was that it was difficult enough to attract media interest, so every little bit helped...

In 1998, when the world was at their feet, Cerys remarked that no matter the circumstances surrounding their meeting, "I really thought all this would happen, I've thought that ever since I met up with Mark."

Importantly, Cerys has always maintained the utmost faith in Mark's ability as a writer. She always possessed a strong belief in their songwriting and musical abilities and their determination to develop an original sound.

The duo started their busking days on the streets in Cardiff city centre, performing weird songs to anyone passing by, seemingly as high as kites and often playing in differing keys and tempos.

A certain amount of naivety in street politics didn't help their cause. In addition to performing music, a knowledge of the streets and how to obtain a fixed pitch are key requisites. This was new territory for them and they were unfamiliar with the ground rules that necessitated perseverance and a preparedness to deal.

After twelve months or so, Cerys and Mark quit busking, but they continued to write songs and dreamt of the future. Their early songs were about the tribulations of love, life, and sex; the same areas of personal politics that were to feature heavily in Catatonia's future repertoire.

Mark considered that their main aim was to get a "beautiful tune and try not to be too predictable with it". Avoiding writing songs from personal experience because, "they'd be pretty fucking boring", what surprises many, who just see Cerys as a vocalist, is that she wrote a lot of the music.

As their confidence grew, they decided to rehearse a few songs at the Grass Roots in Cardiff, then a cheap studio that doubled as a youth centre for kids with problems, or without money.

They persisted and started playing local venues such as The Yellow Kangaroo pub – a venue so small it would now struggle to accommodate Catatonia's road crew – and the Clwb Ifor Bach. Their first appearance at the latter was memorable in that they managed to complete their set at all, the state they were in, Cerys having made serious inroads into the Clwb's stock of brandy to steady her nerves.

They had no specific management as such but there is a close-knit cama-
raderie in Welsh music circles. Huw Williams and his partner Natasha
Hale encouraged them in these early days. Huw was then in a band called
the Poo Sticks and Cerys' voice had caught the attention of Natasha.

In recognition of their newly-found songwriting partnership, Mark and
Cerys thought they should adopt special names. Mark Roberts became
Mark E Zaun and Cerys Matthews became Cerys Ananzapela. Ananzapela
was Cerys' childhood imaginary friend. (These imaginary names lasted
briefly for the two singles released through Crai.)

Realising that they had potential, they decided to persevere and form a
group. Legend has it that the advertisement ran as follows: 'Three gullible
tossers required to make up dodgy beat combo... Laundry skills a must.
Do you like Mud?'

I have not confirmed the existence of this advert, consigning it to one
of those apocryphal stories regarding the band's early years. Aled had obvi-
ously also heard the story at a later date, because he said he thought it
meant mud (sludgy stuff) as opposed to the seventies pop group of "Tiger
Feet" fame. Whether the advert appeared or not, they eventually recruited
Paul Jones (bass), Clancy Pegg (keyboards) and Dafydd Ieuan (drums).
Dafydd tried for a couple of years to drum for both Catatonia and Super
Furry Animals.

It was Cerys who asked Mark if Clancy could join to add keyboards to
the band. This put Mark in a tight spot, as Clancy was there when Cerys
asked. He agreed. His decision was a musical one, but if Cerys and Clancy
both kicked off together, then the Welsh Guards would have a struggle to
contain them.

As with the origin of most outfits, the numbers and individual members
of Catatonia were flexible during this period. While the group was being
put together they would meet up in the City Arms in Cardiff and dream
about sex and drugs and rock 'n' roll. They planned their escape from their
situation and drank themselves into oblivion. Cerys was on the dole and
desperate not to keep seeing the remains of her Giro at the bottom of the
glass or down the toilet.

"We knew we wanted to be in a band," she explained, "and we knew we
wanted it to be different... I know it sounds like a silly cliché, but we actually wanted to find new sounds and tunes."

The origin of the name of the band came from an Aldous Huxley book
The Doors of Perception. It was adopted shortly after Mark and Cerys retired
from busking. They were both quite drunk and thought that Catatonia

meant something like nirvana. Cerys considers that the dictionary they used to check out the word must have been quite optimistic and that they are erroneously named. Initially, they played as Sweet Catatonia, but swiftly abandoned the adjective.

Driven by ambition they set about playing gigs anywhere they could, charging around from venue to venue in a Transit van. Touring like mules was something they would do for the next few years in search of the prize that would one day be theirs.

They played at places in the valleys and throughout South and West Wales and even ventured further afield when bookings became available. One London venue, the 100 Club, was a popular gig for them. Outdoor concerts, such as Plaid Cymru-organised events, also followed.

As a result of their gigging, enlivened by Cerys' regular politically incorrect comments, Catatonia soon gained a loyal following. They had a good fan-base in Wales and rapidly acquired growing English and continental support – despite insisting that they were a "bumbling crew".

For Cerys this was a new experience – the others had all been in bands before – but she was openly enthusiastic about playing all these venues. She had the utmost faith in her fellow band members and felt that being in Catatonia was already "the biggest love in my life." This enthusiasm and passion endured despite having to overcome the innumerable petty problems that would have discouraged most bands. In the early days they did all the wrong things, but the consolation for them was that all their mates in other bands learnt from their mistakes. As with a lot of groups just starting out, payment, if any, was minimal. Many a time, they struggled to break even. On one occasion they even had to borrow money off a fan to pay the toll on the Severn Bridge to get home.

Having already played in Europe, more continental bookings were readily accepted, with Brittany in particular being a popular destination. Welsh and Breton are very similar languages and Welsh bands and Breton bands often participated in gig exchanges. It was all very relaxed. Sometimes there'd be 14-year-old school kids organising concerts and groups would show up in cars and vans sharing each other's equipment. Sometimes there was no PA system, so it was a case of making do with whatever was there. It was a far cry from the pampered set-up of many of today's manufactured bands.

For Catatonia themselves, just being in a band was success enough, anything else was just a welcome bonus. It is a philosophy that still prevails. They temper any thoughts of continuing success with the fact that, "We've

always done what we fancied." If the volatile music industry cold-shoul-
dered them, then so be it.

However, they were beginning to garner interest from within the industry. One of their English gigs in Tufnell Park was witnessed by Rough
Trade founder Geoff Travis, who was later to sign them for Blanco Y Negro.
"When I first saw them they had a keyboard player, they were less coherent
then," he commented. But at least he had remembered them as a band to
watch for the future.

Along with her changing lifestyle, Cerys was already aware of what the
media was capable of. "When I started being in a band, I told my mother
that everything I say and do would be beyond my control, and anyway it
would all be lies controlled by outside forces. She knows that everything I
do is blessed with good intentions."

Her voice was already beginning to attract attention, because even then
there was a unique edge to her vocals. But it could still be fragile, something that Cerys was all too aware of, and as a result she practised and practised. As a band, Catatonia already had their own distinctive, individual
sound, albeit an amalgam of driving rock, lilting Celtic ballads and emotionally charged pop. The varied range of their repertoire was within the
compass of their singer, and highlighted her improving vocal strength and
development. Their new material nurtured Cerys' voice rather than force-
fed it.

Self-belief is a powerful tool and Cerys had already travelled a long way
from the days of busking on Queen Street, Cardiff, where the wind-chill
factor would freeze a brothel Madame's knickers to her nether regions.

At this time there was an added bonus for the developing talent in Wales.
In the early nineties, the television company S4C realised the importance
of youth programmes and decided to put local bands on their shows. So
Catatonia, Gorky's Zygotic Mynci and Super Furry Animals, amongst
others, were given money to go into the studios and even make videos.

A bonding developed between these three groups that is still very much
in place. They would organise and promote their own gigs in bars, with
no manager or agent involved, thus allowing everybody to focus on their
music. As well as encouragement from S4C, the Welsh speaking music
scene was also subsidised by the Welsh Language Society who then helped
bands put on gigs, supplied PAs and did posters, etc.

"I was bilingual," explains Cerys. "I never came across contemporary
Welsh language music until I was eighteen, so initially it sounded really

odd, and we'd sing in English as well because I wanted to be as successful
as Shirley Bassey. That was my condition for getting involved."

To some extent there is a self-sufficiency about the way music in Wales
works. Cardiff-based Ankst Music released a fifth anniversary compilation
tape cassette "A P Elvis" on April 8th 1993, featuring Catatonia singing
"Gwen". It is a song of intricate beauty even though it has had nearly as
many titles as one Charles Windsor (having recorded it as "Gwen", "Gyda
Gwen" and "New Mercurial Heights"). The tune never fails to bring a
lump to my throat.

* * *

However, while Catatonia were setting out on their forward trail and
things were beginning to happen for the group, some 200 miles away I
was going in the other direction. I had been retired on the grounds of ill-
health because I was struggling to cope with my terminally ill wife.

Debbie was my second wife. We became engaged three weeks after meeting, lived together from then on and married some years later. She was a
very vibrant, OTT lady, and her personality would have given Cerys' a run
for its money.

When she was told she had Krukenberg's tumour in her ovaries and that
she had at most six months to live, we were both devastated. On returning
home from hospital she telephoned those who needed to know and told
me to get ready for the wildest six months of my life. If she had to go,
she was going in a blaze of glory. Typical of her, she battled on for eight
months longer than the six-month death sentence.

Debbie informed people that she had one of the rarest forms of cancer.
"I'm special you see, not your common or garden rubbish for me," she
would boast.

During one of her medical examinations they discovered that in the past
her appendix had become infected and had adhered itself to her womb.
Could she remember when that was? She informed them that she had had
a gippy tummy a couple of years previously. She had gone through the
pain threshold and had never let on. Whoever said women are the weaker
sex obviously has never met one.

In our last meaningful conversation some weeks before she died, I
remember saying to her "I'm losing you aren't I?" Her reply was to the
point. "Thank fuck you've realised that. I've been hanging on through all
this pain because you couldn't accept it."

She then bollocked me for always putting other people first, at the expense of doing what I really wanted to do, and she made me promise to follow whatever destiny had in store for me.

Destiny! What is destiny?

The answer to me was to follow my instincts without question. I would realise my objectives irrespective of the consequences. But that was to manifest itself some troubled years later.

Within a couple of months of losing her I suffered a sub-arachnoid brain haemorrhage – which was not related to what I had gone through. When I was discharged I asked a few questions and was told that up to a few years previously, I would have just been left to die. Only a very small percentage ever survived this particular type of haemorrhage and many remained in a very disabled state. I have nothing but the highest praise for my local health centre and everyone at the hospital in Sheffield.

So, how did I repay their efforts?

By trying to kill myself.

Within a couple of months of my coming out of hospital, my mother died from secondary cancer. She was from coal-mining stock and she too must have gone through hell disguising the pain she was in. She made the seven mile round journey on public transport to visit me every day I was in hospital, completely unaware of the severity of her own illness.

My world had collapsed around me. I was put on anti-depressants but they only aggravated my condition. All the drugs I was given seemed to be hallucinogenic. I saw objects disappearing through walls and I knew they weren't there, yet I was compelled to follow them with the obvious consequences. At one stage my face was flatter than an owl's.

Some of the drugs gave me violent irritations of the skin that caused me to continuously scratch myself. On numerous occasions I would have more skin under my fingernails than on parts of my body.

I wanted out.

The five weeks I was in hospital have been the only days since my 14th birthday that I did not consume alcohol. That is not a boast, it is something that I am neither proud nor ashamed of. It is just a fact. But it did play a major role in influencing my next decision.

To hasten my exit, I started really hitting the booze. I was doing a bottle of Jack Daniels and a bottle of Hungarian Bull's Blood red wine a day at home, plus everything I could drink in the pubs and that included the dregs from glasses brought back to the bar. If I didn't die from drink, I would surely walk in front of a bus, or fall off a cliff.

Self-respect, dignity, pride, I pissed them all against the wall. I would wake up screaming because I had actually woken up at all. The empty bottles cluttering my bedroom resembled dead soldiers who had given their all in my own battle campaign for death.

Why was I alive? Everything I had had was dead – why the fuck wasn't I?

It is little wonder that I found support and friendship at home rapidly disappearing.

My trademark jester's suit was hung in the wardrobe for what would be several fraught years. For the only time in my life, I was to wear the heavy, dark cloak of despair.

Some friends I had in Wales offered me breathing space. It seemed they were concerned about me. Unfortunately I didn't share the same care.

My friends liked a drink but did not share my passion for music. They took me all over South and West Wales, dropped me off wherever music was being performed, went to the pubs of their choice and then literally picked me up and took me back. Basically, they knew salvation was in my own hands. If all else failed, like it was intended to, then they could take care of the necessary arrangements.

I must have heard scores of artists and bands during that dark period, and no disrespect to any of them, nothing registered with me. Then, one alcohol-soaked night I heard, but didn't see, a band that caught my attention. I listened carelessly, but with great feeling, I reacted.

"You fucking bastards!"

I was stood behind what looked like the Llanelli front row. They turned, looked me up and down, and chose to ignore me. I probably looked damaged enough already. The comment wasn't aimed at them, but they weren't to know that. What I knew, even in the state I was in, was that I had experienced my first positive vibe in many a month.

I do not know which song grabbed me. My subconscious and body reactions since indicate "Gyda Gwen", but I will never know. Somehow, unwittingly and unknowingly, I had stumbled across what was to prove to be the key to my salvation.

A couple of days later, when I could string a sentence together, I told my friends of this. They found out who the band were and took me to two more of their gigs.

I refused to look at the band, something I tried to maintain, albeit unsuccessfully, for the next couple of years. I had to trust my ears, it had to be aural. I did not even recall their name, I found it difficult to remember my own.

From the bottom of the darkest pit, destiny was offering me a way out. Music was throwing me a lifeline, Catatonia were providing the lifeboat.

Generally I am reluctant to praise, being a very cynical Yorkshireman by nature. Only three bands have ever held my attention for any length of time. I followed the Beatles from 1962 to 1969 until I finally became fed up with Yoko Ono's influence, and the Rolling Stones from 1963 to 1969 until my idol Brian Jones was taken from us. I was absolutely certain that I was never again going to come across anything that would capture my attention so profoundly as these two groups had done.

As I had grown older disgracefully, whenever I assessed a band it was viewed with a "seen it all before" attitude.

Thank God I was to be proved wrong.

When I happened upon Catatonia, I tried my hardest not to succumb. At the time, I was a difficult person to communicate with, almost impossible, and whatever it was musically that drew me to them, I did not know. If anything touches my soul it evokes within me an irresistible passion, but my passion is not blind. My objectivity becomes more focussed, my criticism sharper.

When I returned to Sheffield, my doctor thought I might have gone too far down the line. It was up to my mind and my body to respond to any new positive impulses. Apparently I was now a bystander. The damage had been done. The next few months would determine whether I lived or died.

On my better days, I knew I had to help myself. Virtually straight away I cut out my drinking at home. Surprisingly, this did not prove difficult. The hard part was stopping drinking to excess in pubs and clubs. This took me several years to control. Some people still think I drink too much and they may be right. However, what I drink now, I would have called breakfast between 1993 and 1996.

On regular visits to Wales, people who really had no reason to, gave me tremendous support. Most of them didn't know me, but I ended up loving each and every one of them. I visited many places. If there was to be no hope then at least I could have a last journey of discovery. I felt a hypocrite... I had slagged this country off time and time again. Why shouldn't I? It is an English national sport after all! So why was I falling in love with the most beautiful thing in the world – Wales?

My only previous connection with music and Wales had been supporting Bolsterstone Male Voice Choir as a solo folk singer, when they played
a few concerts in the South Yorkshire area, shortly after they had won the
International Choir section at the Llangollen Eisteddfod. (Alright, I own
up, I did buy some Amen Corner records as well.)

I now took in as many Catatonia gigs as I could and also saw a lot more
local bands. My attempt at recovery was slowly starting, and I could only
hope to repair the self-inflicted wounds and damage.

I was the key player in my destiny.

* * *

Enter a key player in the fortunes of Catatonia. Rhys Mwyn runs Crai
Records, an offshoot of Wales' original record label Sain. He says, "I started
working with Catatonia through knowing Mark and Cerys when the original demos emerged. The plan was that I was going to give them a hand to
see if they could get some record company interest. There wasn't really any
at that stage, because it was just before the Manics had broken through,
so there were only a few people who would give us the time of day. It
wasn't as easy as it is now. I think it was Mark's idea to do a couple of
singles through Crai just to get something out. Obviously their aim was
to get a record deal and I think they realised that they needed a couple of
independent releases to get that. About two years of my time was focussed
on Catatonia."

Their first release on Crai, the *For Tinkerbell* EP, was released in September 1993 and was made Single of the Week by *New Musical Express*. The
Catatonia line up was unchanged at this stage. Matthews and Roberts had
written all the songs and the production was by the group themselves. The
EP featured "Gyda Gwen", a lilting Celtic melody which still rates as one
of their finest offerings; also a fledgling version of "Sweet Catatonia" (not
yet developed into the later anthemic song). "For Tinkerbell" reminded
me of something that the Beatles might have recorded post *Sergeant Pepper*.
"Dimbran" (which literally means "no crows", though its Welsh lyrics do
not translate into English coherently) presented a perfect Welsh language
vehicle for Cerys' expressive vocals. When singing "Dimbran" at gigs, particularly in England and Scotland, Cerys would frequently dedicate the
song to the Welsh international football team.

Whether or not you were a Welsh language speaker the signals were
going out. Here was a voice that was now commanding attention; here was
a very promising songwriting team; here was Catatonia. They now had a
very creditable record to endorse their ever-growing reputation as a class

live band. With it being released through a small independent company though, it was not accessible to all of their fans. I managed to get a copy but cannot remember how. The single posed no threat to the charts, it wasn't intended to. It was really a showcase of their talents. A sprat to catch a mackerel.

Another outlet appeared when Ankst produced a video compilation, which was released in December 1993. This was entitled *Pop Pethdau* (Pop Things) and Catatonia are featured performing "Difrrycheulid" (Snail Ambition) and "Dimbran". The band was busy performing where they could, but this was still a loose arrangement for several reasons, the major one being Daf playing in two bands.

They continued their own style of gigging, learning more from their mistakes if anything, and in May 1994 Crai released the band's second single for the label. Entitled "Hooked" it featured the same line-up and songwriting combination. Recorded at the same two studios as the first single, it too received the accolade of *New Musical Express* Single of the Week.

"Hooked" is a light plaintive song, pleasant but not outstanding. "Difrycheulyd" demonstrates the band's quirkiness with its bilingual lyrics in Welsh and French. The spiky French comments sung by Mark were taken from a French/English phrase book, he later admitted. If he had not opted for drumming lessons at school he could have saved himself the cost of the phrase book.

"Fall Beside Her" is probably the best song, but still did not reflect the progress that the band were making. The vocals were mellow and appealing, but there were signs at gigs of a more driving energy in the Cerys larynx, which was not captured on disc. Clearly, Cerys had more to offer vocally – the question remained how to release it? Musically, also, Catatonia needed a little more muscle and cohesion.

Issuing singles through Crai was a start, but Cerys in particular was disappointed because family and friends found it difficult to buy these records. "It's sad like, but I can't understand all this ideology about independent music, 'cos it's a bit of an elitist thing."

Unfortunately, without the backing of a major label, it is often a case of releasing records through an independent company, or simply selling or giving away home-produced demos.

I was managing to get to a few of their gigs, but there were just as many occasions when my planned attendance had to be cancelled due to my health problems. Nowadays, I refer to them as my "black holes", but I never knew when the bouts of depression were going to happen.

Specific events or sad thoughts did not trigger them off. They just descended when I least expected them. I would close all the curtains and just lay down until I could function. It was a weird sensation. Rather than fight it, I relied on it to devour itself. These spells could last from a few hours to a few days. 1993–1994 was the worst period for me, and then things began to slowly improve.

I felt I was walking on eggshells. For once in my life I was solitary. It would have been unfair of me to expect anyone to go down that road with me. Occasionally, I would feel like my old self, but there was always the possibility of my falling backwards. Overall, I felt as much use as a one-legged man in an arse-kicking competition.

One thing that I was now recognising was that a vacancy had occurred on the top of my head, which was once occupied by a flowing blond mane. Whether it was the after-effects of my brain operation, or the rewards of a life of debauchery, I had no idea. People were now in the habit of saying things like "Friar Tuck" to me. Well, it sounded something like that. Hopefully my reputation was not catching up with me.

Catatonia themselves had started getting a bit of a reputation by sheer perseverance and by releasing singles on obscure labels, even though they had no management and there was no thriving Welsh music scene as yet.

"We got one gig in London at the Splash Club," Cerys explained, "which you get paid for in coupons or vouchers and you don't make any money – you lose money."

Two of their better local gigs at this time, the Roc Y Cnapan and The Eisteddfod in Llanelwedd reinforced the band's status as fast rising talents. Fortunately a gig promoter, Paul Buck, had seen Catatonia and took the band on. (He was later to become the agent for Big Leaves, formerly Beganifs – friends of Catatonia.)

Their name was then passed onto to MRM, who subsequently became the band's management. This resulted in more gigs. MRM, however, made little secret of the fact that they were reluctant for Clancy to continue in the band. One member of MRM, Richard Lowe, had previously worked with Rough Trade and knew Geoff Travis, so the wheels were put in motion to persuade him that Catatonia were worth taking on.

So, in late August, 1994 another record, "Whale" was released on 7" vinyl by the Rough Trade Singles Club. It featured "Whale" which is an English language version of "Gwe", and "You Can" (a high quality B-side). Again it was *NME* Single of the Week.

"You Can" is an effortless song which incorporates the word "recumbent" and was about balancing fantasy with reality; less about wanting to be adored, more about learning to respect yourself. The last time I saw them perform it was at the 1996 Reading Festival.

By now, the band was on the road more than double yellow lines. They continued playing wherever they could, even turning up at gigs in remote parts of Wales only to be told by clueless promoters that they had to buy tickets for their road crew.

In the early days Mark made significant contributions to interviews and in late 1994 he claimed that Catatonia were bigger than the Manic Street Preachers in Wales, primarily because the Manics rarely played there anymore.

At an early September gig in Manchester, following the release of "Whale", Catatonia celebrated yet another *NME* Single of the Week with a few pre-show drinks. Cerys was displaying her regular fashion look, wearing sunglasses on stage whilst she played guitar and sang. The fact that this was a cellar bar and the band were worse the wear for drink resulted in lyrics being screwed, guitar chords miss-hit, and introductions slurred, as Cerys wobbled unsteadily on her feet. The vision of them celebrating any future chart success became a fascinating prospect.

No wonder one critic described them, as, "like an explosion in a knife and fork factory." The music industry was not to be put off. The gigging continued all over Britain, including several more disasters in London.

"We played the Monarch," recalls Paul, "and there were loads of record companies there to see us. We'd been on the piss all day and it was a long day as well. Then you're bundled on stage, and it's like 'What the fuck am I going to do with this guitar?' It was a very fast gig, I remember that much. After a couple of lines you don't give a fuck anyway. But I remember seeing a lot of bemused faces in the audience."

In 1998, Cerys explained their earlier pedestrian career development and admitted that they had made the slowest progress of any band she knew.

If the band was playing an out of town gig where A&R people were going to attend, they made sure all their equipment was set up by the middle of the afternoon. This left them with nothing to do, so they drank the time away. By the time they took to the stage they would be absolutely paralytic and play a poor set, so it was back to square one.

In addition to gigging, they were also active in the recording studios whenever they had the opportunity and a further Catatonia release "Dream On" formed part of an 18-track compilation on *Volume* issue 12, in the winter of 1994. The song itself was played regularly at gigs right up to the *International Velvet* tour of 1998, and Cerys lists it as one of her favourite Catatonia songs.

As interest was now growing, people wanted more information and naturally the band found themselves being interviewed by curious journalists. In some of these early media sessions (1994-95), their press officer ensured that the band members had an ample supply of free booze, along with a supply of fictitous adventures for publicity, such as Cerys being pestered by a French stalker at a gig in Cardiff. One interviewer likened their music to "short but epic fourth generation rock songs pitched somewhere between the peaks of *Rubber Soul* Beatles, the serene plains of *Sonic Flower Groove* by Primal Scream, and the wasted lows of The Nymphs."

Regarding comparisons, "I think you should know your limitations, and then ignore them and go ahead and do what the fuck you want to anyway," commented Mark. Cerys was more to the point, "We're the best tunesmiths of the nineties. Proper tunes, original tunes, tunes that will spook you, tunes that will seduce you. You'll go to hell and back with Catatonia." In my case, that was a most prophetic statement indeed.

By the end of 1994, the music world was beginning to take guarded notice of the band. Catatonia were now on the way towards gaining recognition further afield than the land of their fathers. They were getting the taste, but there were many other equally aspiring artists following the yellow brick road to the Emerald city of pop stardom. However, in Catatonia's case, their own little Dorothy was playing guitar as well as supplying the vocals. Oh! for a Tin Man to cross their path, and help them on their journey.

JUMP OR BE SANE

I always thought we were successful, even when we were selling bugger all.
Cerys Matthews

A fan of a band rarely considers the possibility of a change in their line-up. Why should they? The reason you are a fan is stood on stage in front of you, or is to be heard singing into your headphones as you relax. If there is a change in personnel then there is no guarantee that they will still hold your affection. This happened to me when Brian Jones was dumped from the Rolling Stones.

I loved the music of this Welsh band, yet I still did not know much about them. It had taken me this long to even come to terms with the singer's name. I had progressed from thinking her name was a squiggle on a piece of paper, to calling her "the lady with the guitar". Now I understood that she was Cerys, but in my confused state, I did not know what a "Cerys" was. We didn't have one in Sheffield.

People in my home city kept asking which record label was this Welsh outfit signed to and had they been on radio or TV? When I replied that they released through independent labels, the hand gestures I received indicated I was a wanker.

By 1995 I was becoming used to following Catatonia and all that it entailed. I had not considered the fact that I was a fan. The music and the band were in the process of assisting my recovery and that was just enough for me to handle then.

At indoor gigs I could still only watch or listen from a distance, often not even in the same room. The number of venues that thought they had discovered a ghost, only to find me secreting myself from the band, was steadily growing. At some places I was about as welcome as a pin in a condom factory.

I was now very familiar with the bus and railway stations of the UK as I no longer drove a car. If they awarded a university degree in missing transport connections, I would graduate with honours. Logic was not my strongpoint at this time, so when National Express explained that to go to Lincoln from Sheffield on one of their coaches (a journey that is east bound), entailed me changing coaches at Leicester, (which is very much south bound), I did not question it. The fact that I could have walked to Lincoln and back in the time it took the coaches only became apparent to me a couple of years later.

My father was a man of few words; it took him over twenty years to spit out, "Will you marry me?" to my mother. However, when he did speak he conveyed great sense. He told me that everything can be taken apart and examined, but even if you could put it back together, it would never be the same. That was the reason I dared not attempt to break down what it was that made the band so special to me. I could not afford to lose the lifeline. It takes a hell of a battle to overcome depression, many people have not been half as fortunate as myself. I regarded Catatonia with the same feelings that someone who has been saved from drowning has for their rescuer, it is like a one-way bonding.

The actual journeys to the gigs, and the people I met there, very gradually helped me regain my self-confidence and self-respect, almost as much as the pleasure of the gigs themselves.

Relying on word of mouth to find out where the band was playing though was a problem. There were a number of times that I was told in good faith where and when they would be playing, only to arrive and find I was a few days too early or too late. I turned up in Aberystwyth one day to find out from some reliably informed fan that I was actually in the wrong country. Catatonia were gigging in Paris!

Ah, the joys of the jungle telegraph.

I usually gained compensation by watching whoever else was playing in the area. Generally, the timetable cock-ups were in Wales, so I was able to indulge in my growing love of Welsh bands. The music press, however, still seemed to find it hard to accept that the Principality could produce musicians and singers of quality.

Something else I was noticing was the effect of the Welsh language and accent on myself. Like Gomez from *The Addams Family*, made amorous by Morticia speaking in French, I find the sexiest voice in the world is a Welsh lady either speaking Welsh, or speaking English with a Welsh accent. There is a unique lilt and tonal quality in their voices.

* * *

In 1995 the band charted for the first time, reaching the dizzy heights of number 102 with "Bleed" which was released in February on the Nursery label in CD format and 7" vinyl (limited edition of 1,000). B-sides were "This Boy Can't Swim" and "Painful" (CD only). It also got into the Indie top ten, outselling Elastica's record "Connection" in many shops. This minor achievement was not lost on their fanbase. It was like a non-league club progressing into the First Round of the FA Cup.

This was followed on February 12th by recording "Black Session, Studio 105" in Paris for Bernard Lenoir (France's equivalent to Mark Radcliffe) of which you can still get bootleg copies. (It contains "For Tinkerbell", "Beautiful Sailor", "Bleed", "Mickey", "You Can", "Way Beyond Blue", "This Boy Can't Swim", "Sweet Catatonia" and "Acapulco Gold".) During this period of their career they occasionally spent some of their leisure time in the august company of Monsieur Lenoir.

The band then returned to make their first demos at Grass Roots studios. It boasted a 16-track studio and was only £50 per day. "It's still going," says Owen, "only now it's 24-track. It's got a programming room as well." The last time I visited these studios there was a press cutting there recalling Catatonia's recording session.

"Bleed" had gained them some publicity in the music trade, but another activity seemed to be whetting the appetites of most hacks. Attention was focussing on the drinking exploits of Ms Matthews. A reporter had written of Cerys that she was only adhering to the healthy rule observed by all smart women. "Ten pints of fizzy lager a day helps to keep boring doctors away."

Whilst only some of the stories are true, Cerys feels they are no different to any of the nonsense that anybody gets up to when they go drinking. "I enjoy a drink but then so do a lot of other people," she admitted. "I love my alcohol, it's the best drug known to man."

Cerys is excitable and admits to being "a bit of a fool when I'm out", although she insists she is trying to be more refined, but this is going to be a long process. Perhaps the compromise of getting pissed on champagne rather than strong lager is the solution.

"Besides, it's not the drinking, it's the thirst," she explains. "We were brought up on Maxi Homebrew, which is this brewing kit popular in Wales, which only uses the purest ingredients, and there's Peculiar Welsh Whisky." The drinking exploits, real and fictitious, were to continue to haunt the band.

Meanwhile, more Catatonia material was released when Ankst issued two compilation EPs entitled *S4C Makes Me Want To Smoke Crack – Volumes 1 and 2*. The hardest one to obtain now is Volume 1, which features Catatonia singing "Cariadon Ffol". There were only 500 vinyl copies pressed.

By now the music world was taking the band more seriously and they were interviewed by *Melody Maker* in March. In the interview Cerys predicted that a new wave of fascinating groups would appear from South Wales and her prophecy was proved accurate. She felt that bands in Wales had been left alone for so long and that this had given everybody time to develop into great imaginative outfits such as Gorkys and Super Furry Animals. "See, out here we know all about sheep," she laughed "we can learn from their mistakes."

The subject of their Welsh nationality and language was a popular target for interviewers. Certainly, the media were struggling to cope with the fact that there was talent in Wales, even though 'it was not as we know it'. Some journos wrote about it as if they had discovered the missing link.

Catatonia had championed non-conformist ways of approaching the press, which gave the them a hook to hang their interviews on. Cerys demonstrated from the outset that she was not going to be a bimbo. She would give each question the answer it deserved, often taking the interview to the reporter.

"What are the Welsh famous for?" she would ask. "Three things; sheep-shagging, drunks, and rugby. And that's what I've had my reputation as being a drunk built on, and I'm not."

But like them or not, things were beginning to go their way. They possessed an aura that would eventually earn them a deal with a major league record company.

Rough Trade's Geoff Travis, now Managing Director of Blanco Y Negro, signed them up in April for the WEA-backed label. The advance was reputed to be £350,000 – although financial disclosures in the music business are not noted for their accuracy.

"They are quite unique," Travis said. "What stands out is the quality songwriting and Cerys' voice, which has real soul. Their new work demonstrates the virtues of playing a lot. I should have signed them a year ago because I love them, and it would have been a lot cheaper."

This is where I have to declare that I have a degree in management, and have worked in management and music all my life, though not always simultaneously. I have never, nor would ever, ask any member of Catatonia or their management about their joint working relationship. That would be totally unethical, it is their private business. I only inform you of this, so that you will appreciate some of the comments and questions I pose from now on, and why certain things have puzzled me.

Signing to a label is obviously a major boost to any band or artist, but it generally adds another layer of management because the label understandably wants to protect and develop its investment.

True to form, the band celebrated in the pub until well past closing time. It was a requirement that Cerys was to fulfil several promotional duties the following morning, but she found herself too ill to speak. Her hangover lasted for days.

A few months and several hangovers later, Cerys assessed the new working arrangements. Having been used to doing everything themselves and learning from their mistakes, it came as a culture shock for the band to have other people involved and working for them. Initially, Cerys found it difficult to adjust to not being the first to know about things and it caused her to lose her temper from time to time. Being a loner, and quite stubborn, she would probably be the first to admit that she is not the easiest person to manage.

The upside of it all was that the deal provided them with enough funds to allow them to travel to gigs in comfort and stop over in hotels afterwards rather than having to drive back to Cardiff. Cerys put it in a football analogy, "We're getting there now. We're ready for the European Cup." It was time to show everyone that here was a proper band.

One opportunity came when Catatonia were asked to play a prestigious showcase event for the music industry called *In The City*. Bands submit application forms and specify their range of music. The lucky ones are invited to play in the city selected to host the event. There are venues for all categories and the various sections of the music trade come and pass judgement. In 1995 the city was Manchester.

In what was turning out to be a familiar course of events, the band's performance suffered greatly as a result of Cerys going on a bender before the gig. Their new label must have been having serious doubts about the band's marketability. Would they ever deliver what they were capable of when it mattered? With hindsight they should have signed Cerys' mother in an advisory capacity to give her daughter a parental slap when necessary. No matter what condition a group arrives on stage, the audience always notices the singer, (particularly if the singer is female – even in these times) and rightly or wrongly they carry the can for the group. There were times when it seemed that Catatonia had developed a knack of preventing their talents reaching a wider audience. It was frustrating too for those who followed the band. Even though I was far from being a star-struck kid, I also prayed that they would not self-destruct.

Evidence that Catatonia really were capable of making headway when they put their minds to it came in July when they performed at the Phoenix Festival. It was a special day for Cerys as this was the first festival she had ever attended. The band played a good set, however most of the crowd seemed unaware of Catatonia as they performed in one of the tents. This was just as well as it was pouring with rain. (A weather jinx appears to follow me to outdoor festivals.)

While they had squandered several key opportunities to achieve a breakthrough, the band still retained an ability to charm the punters. People had a sense of belonging with Catatonia. A Catatonia gig could be like a night out with your mates… and still is.

Gareth Thomas of Baglan, a fan of the band, has memories of these early times. He'd been active in the music scene around South Wales since being a member of a band in Port Talbot in the punk years of the late 1970s. He had made the acquaintance of Mark, then of Y Cyrff, so when the latter's new band came to the small Barons Nightclub in Swansea, he went along to check them out and meet up with old friends.

He did not know their material and was initially not too impressed. He recalls that the people running the concert were handing out cassettes of the group's material and that most of the audience had a copy. He carried on drinking and chatting and decided that if the band grew on him then he would obtain a copy over the following weeks, but as is often the case in these situations he never managed to acquire one.

In 1998, he met up with the organiser of the gig and it took some prompting before he could remember the tapes, but alas he did not have any stored away. Of such things is the *Antiques Roadshow* made.

Come the autumn, work began on Catatonia's debut album which was to be entitled *Way Beyond Blue*. Armed with gallons of cash 'n' carry booze they adjourned to the Maison Rouge Studios in South West London to work with producer Stephen Street. It was not going to be the sort of album that could be produced to a set timetable. In fact, many studios would eventually feature in recording the album, which would not be released for another twelve months. This delay allowed tracks to be laid down and released as singles before the album was completed. Catatonia insisted that it was to be called a pop album and not indie music, as they were usually tagged.

Major radio exposure followed, when in October the band recorded a Mark Radcliffe session for Radio 1, ostensibly to promote the release of a new single "Sweet Catatonia" in the new year. The session included "Sweet Catatonia", "You Can" (a.k.a. "Message"), "Infantile", and "Acapulco Gold" and also featured an interview.

A demonstration of Catatonia's growing global appeal was hinted at when Nursery released an album in Japan in November entitled *The Sublime Magic Of (The Songs 1994-1995)*. It featured "Cariadon Ffol", "Bleed", "This Boy Can't Swim", "Painful", "Dream On", "Whale", "You Can", "Hooked", "Fall Beside Her" and "Difrycheulid". Available now in the UK only as an expensive import, it is probably worth the money.

However, things inside the Catatonia camp were not going smoothly. Dafydd, who had been trying to drum with two groups finally left the band to join the Super Furries full-time after they signed a record deal with Creation. He recommended as his replacement a drummer who he had met years earlier at a summer camp with the Welsh Youth Society – Aled Richards.

Of more concern was the bitterness that had developed between Cerys and Clancy. You would want either of these ladies on your side in an argument. In many ways they were similar but there were also very stark contrasts. The arguments got more intense and the rivalry – call it what you will – strained relationships and friendships within the band. Consequently MRM got their wish and Clancy left.

In a 1998 interview Cerys put it rather curtly by saying, "We used to have a keyboard player who was a girl. We had to get rid of her 'cos me and her were fighting all the time."

"Vying for our attention," interjects Mark. "It's alright having a girl in the band, but we get ticked off every now and then."

On a purely selfish and personal basis, I didn't really want to consider the possibility that the band might split up permanently. At that time I still needed the lifeline that Catatonia represented. I was slowly coping with my depression, but I was far from clear. It was still a case of going one step forwards and sometimes two steps back. I existed by setting targets and when I reached one target, I set another. My support was the music of Catatonia and a growing love for Wales. Between them they had dragged me part way out of the hole I was in, but there was still a fair way to go if I was to make it.

When I used to sing in a band, I would knock back a half-pint of gin in one go before going on stage to sing. If we did two spots, it was repeated. On rare occasions, we played three spots (especially if it was a Working Men's Club and we were playing in between games of bingo.) I was told on these occasions that we were very good – I haven't a clue because on those nights I was on a different planet. From inside my depression and drinking, the news of any discord in Catatonia immediately became a three-spot problem.

Following the departure of Clancy, Owen Powell who had been guitar technician, became the last member to join the line-up. This allowed Cerys to put down her guitar.

"We improved when I took off the guitar and gave it someone who could play. This is the big change in the band, I used to play all the time," she graciously admitted. From now on, they were to gain a successful reputation wherever they played.

The jigsaw was complete. Centre stage was now given to "The Voice". Without the trappings of her guitar, not only would she be able to give full rein to her rapidly developing vocal talents, but she could also turn her attention to perfecting the stage presence that is now such a familiar part of Catatonia's show.

If Owen thought he would escape the banter, he was mistaken. Cerys used to taunt him about his previous band called U Thant, whose claim to fame was that their drummer, Frog, put in so much effort that he would collapse at the end of the show. Add to that the pink lurex catsuits and silver hats. Well, you get the picture.

"Thank God they never made it, eh?" teased Cerys.

"Yeah," answered Owen

"Weren't you in that band, Owen?" Cerys put the knife in.

"I wasn't there during the bloody pink-catsuit years," he retorted.

(Frog, incidentally, has valid claims to be the first drummer to play with Catatonia before Dafydd joined up. He would later play drums in the band Crac, of which Clancy was also a member. He and Clancy still toyed with playing in the same group following the demise of Crac at the end of 1999.)

There was still more recorded material to come from Catatonia in 1995. The Welsh label, Ankst, who have assisted many Welsh acts, released another compilation cassette in December. Called *Triskedekaphilia* (the love of the number thirteen – because of the number of songs on the tape) it was a showcase of the Welsh talent that was around at the time.

Catatonia supplied two songs – "Gwe" which is a Welsh language version of "Whale" and "Iago M". The songs on the compilation were recorded for the *Heno Bydd Yr Adar Yn Canu (Tonight The Birds Are Singing)* sessions for the BBC Radio Cymru programme *Hwyrach! (Later)* presented by Nia Melville.

It had turned out to be a good year for the group, and there was really only one way for the year to finish – release another record. So, Catatonia produced a limited edition white vinyl single (1,000 copies) distributed free of charge to the Catatonia mailing list. It contained the tracks "Blow The Millennium Blow" and "Beautiful Sailor". Unsurprisingly, this is now a prized collector's item.

As the band entered 1996 they were in good shape having secured a record deal with Blanco Y Negro, and secured changes in personnel which were to improve the performance and stature of the group. The Tin Man, aka Owen Powell, had crossed their path. Now little Dorothy had ditched her guitar, surely she could lead them to the Emerald City. With the music side tightened up, and the vocalist now able to focus her talents, would Catatonia now go beyond the rainbow?

WAY BEYOND BLUE

Making a noise on stage is what we like doing. And we like making records too.

Cerys Matthews

A voice in the wilderness… That best sums up Catatonia's position in the UK pop scene at the start of 1996, despite their growing reputation. The new line-up had yet to be satisfactorily road-tested, but if it gelled then the prospect of success would be just around the corner. Well, that is what Catatonia thought as threw themselves into the new year.

January 18th saw the release of "Sweet Catatonia" – still a hugely popular song with the fans. It charted at 61 as evidence that tangible progress was being made. The back cover featured Polaroid portraits of the group (Owen had not officially joined the band line-up, but Aled was featured) even though Owen toured to promote the single.

The other tracks on the single were headed up by "Acapulco Gold" followed by "Cut You Inside" (demo) and "Tourist". "Acapulco Gold" is one of Mark's favourite songs. Lasting exactly three minutes, it has a dope referencing title and some neat Spanish guitar playing. "I can't put down why I like it so much," he says. "It's just so, beautiful… It really is too good for a B-side, but the minute we finish writing songs we have to record them, and if there's no album to be done then they're immediately put out as B-sides. We never save them. We never say 'That's too good to be put out right now!'"

The words to "Acapulco Gold", *"When all the dreams subside, they're wrapped in American suicide"* were the first lyrical evidence of the group's feelings toward the USA. Surprisingly the track never found its way onto the *Way Beyond Blue* album.

The video for "Sweet Catatonia" featured the entire band except Owen. It was set in leafy woodland, with little furry animals appearing everywhere causing mayhem. Towards the end of the song, Paul has his head stuck in a beehive. It was inexpensive, pleasant and amusing.

The song broke new ground for the band by reaching the play lists of national daytime radio, giving a pointer that future chart success might be imminent. The band also undertook a tour to promote the single, with Swansea being the appropriate starting point. These gigs concentrated on small to medium sized venues, and allowed them to introduce properly the new line-up. This was to be the forerunner to a series of tours that would see Catatonia spend nearly half the year on the road.

Not surprisingly, when the tour hit Cardiff, the group was in demand. Cerys did a press call in a small back room at Cardiff University Union for over two hours with journalists waiting their turn to question her. An experience she described as being, "Alright… It just feels like I'm in a massage parlour, and that each customer comes in and you offer them your services and you go, 'Blow job £10'".

It was thirsty work for Cerys, (not the blow job, I hasten to add) and the nearby table was cluttered with empty beer bottles. The drink, allied to the fact that she had not yet eaten, was making her feel pissed. She was telling everyone how pleased the band were with the progress they had made, especially now that they were getting radio airplay.

"We've all been doing it a while, and it's fucking ace that we're getting somewhere," she enthused.

Now that they had Owen playing guitar she was convinced the band sounded like it should. Their music at this time was described as "guitars jangling like an entire childhood of Christmas mornings, stuff that bothers you, makes you want its fascinating, frightening pop – jangles and purrs in all the right places. God's own answer to aural sex."

The response Catatonia received from the English-based rock press was certainly an encouragement to Cerys, and she considered that there might now be more emphasis on their music rather than their nationality. She hoped the days of the media taking the piss out of Wales had gone, because, "people from Wales are alright."

Welsh bands have always been wary that if they achieve even a modicum of success then their country and people will disown them. It seems to be a trait of the Celtic races that celebrity is just a day job. When you come back home, remember who you are and where you came from.

"You can only go so far in Wales before people start to resent your success," Owen believes. "I don't know if we've gone so far for people to resent us yet."

"We're on the cusp," commented Mark. "If we have any more success people will hate us, so we want to tread the tightrope – have a bit of success and keep our friends. Not much to ask for, is it?"

Following the tour to promote "Sweet Catatonia" the group kept busy, and the gig list seemed endless. Aberdare Coliseum, on Saturday March 2nd 1996, provided the stage for a concert bill that would now fill most arenas. The band opening the show, the Tragic Love Company, were on the verge of changing their stage name to the Stereophonics and about 50 people were in to see them open the show. Such was their impact that the hall filled up rapidly and by the end of their set the band received a thunderous ovation.

Next on stage were Aberdare's own Pocket Devils, who played to an enthusiastic response from their hometown fans. At the conclusion of their act the audience started to leave gradually, and as it became evident that the headliners Catatonia were seemingly worse the wear for alcohol, the exodus speeded up. The Stereophonics were signed shortly after their performance that night. Cerys admitted, "They did a brilliant gig and we were ruddy awful. They blew us off stage."

In spite of the odd bad gig, the fortunes of the band were rising and April saw the release of "Lost Cat," which charted at 41. On the CD1 version, the B-sides are "All Girls Are Fly" and "Indigo Blind" whilst on CD2 the B-sides are "Sweet Catatonia" (from the Mark Radcliffe live session) and "Whale" (from the Mark Radcliffe live and acoustic session). On the 7" vinyl limited edition the B-side is "To and Fro".

To promote this release, Catatonia undertook a 40-gig tour. Much of their time on the road would be shared with Liverpool band Space, and the groups forged a close friendship.

One gig in particular that stood out for me was at Wolverhampton Supersonic. Offstage at Wolverhampton, I nearly lost it. For some reason my guard was down and my mind was elsewhere. When I mentally returned to this planet, a lady was close to me, smiling – at what I don't know. The lady was Cerys. I dared not speak to her. I have rarely moved so fast. It was disrespectful of me in many ways, but I was still experiencing days when I was very fragile.

Cerys remembers the Birmingham gig on the same tour for completely different reasons. "I did get a pair of Y-fronts thrown at me. They had 'fancy a shag' written on them. I was really pleased about that." I wonder if she recognised the handwriting?

The tour was also notable in that on Wednesday May 1st they played their last gig (to date) at the Clwb Ifor Bach in Cardiff.

Touring with Space was a turning point for Cerys. She was impressed with the way they worked an audience unfamiliar with their music and yet still managed to get results and create a good atmosphere. To her it was another demonstration of the power of music. To watch an unknown band turn an audience round convinced her that she had seen something special. By the summer of 1999, in spite of all the artists she has seen since, nothing has matched this.

Catatonia's newfound status meant hotel luxuries such as jacuzzis and saunas, hot baths and hot rooms. Cerys was not completely taken in by these new surroundings. "My mum bought me a silk lined vanity case to take on our tours. God, if she'd seen some of the places we ended up in."

Paul remained philosophical. He was aware of the need to tour to satisfy the promotional requirements laid down by record companies and agents, but bands need time out to write and record. There had to be a balance struck to satisfy both needs.

The tour itinerary had been so hectic – they had already completed two sell-out national tours – that they reluctantly had to turn down the oppor-tunity to perform at Melody Maker's 70th anniversary party.

On the promotional tour for "Lost Cat", Cerys ended up at a place that was not on the itinerary – Marseilles in the South of France. It was an incident that was to provide the most famous story about her.

Catatonia were due to be interviewed by Everett True of Melody Maker on April 13th in Brighton. Two hours before the interview he received a telephone call from their manager saying Cerys had gone AWOL. The last time she had been sighted, she was blind drunk and on her way to France.

"I went to see the Lightning Seeds three days ago and woke up this morn-ing in Marseilles," explained Cerys, who managed to arrive in time for the interview and the Brighton gig. "I woke up crying. I only went to kill a night and three days later I woke up in France. I'd been drinking champagne in Club class. I had a big plate of aliens last night and threw them all up this morning." Cerys never explained what these "aliens" were and few interviewers were brave enough ever to press her for answers.

Mark was not pleased when Cerys turned up for the interview. He had been so convinced that she would not make it back in time from France, he had bet £30 on it. With hindsight you could be forgiven for thinking this was a publicity stunt. I certainly did. If the management had all this information in advance, as it appears was the case, then in the interests of the band, why was it allowed to develop? Alternatively, this did happen over Cerys' 27th birthday, so perhaps it was a celebratory bash with a difference. On checking this story, the band confirmed it to be true.

At this time, the record company's press officer would regularly fax music magazines with news of the singer's latest drinking escapades and off-stage antics, some true, most false, which would gain more publicity than the records. The list of notorious events is seemingly endless, and for every true one, three more would be invented. Mark declared, "We look at ourselves more as Penelope Pitstop and the Anthill Mob. We're always getting Cerys out of scrapes."

Cerys helped the cause by regularly wearing a band T-shirt with the logo "Fast-rising-lager-soaked-riproaring-poptart." Her unique charisma was already attracting attention, and the signs were that this could be a very marketable commodity.

More stories soon spread about Cerys. These included her cartwheeling the full length of the roof of a bus, the condoning of shoplifting, trying to distract Danni Minogue at a Cardiff pop show by flashing her tits at her, and pissing in dressing room sinks to try and create an overflow.

They once even tried stealing a JCB from a building site that was opposite a police station. Cerys, Mark and Owen climbed into the cab and tried to start it up, but they were unsuccessful. As they jumped over the fence to leave the scene, they saw two policemen hanging out of the station window who had witnessed the whole proceedings. The trio promptly legged it down the street.

One story that the band recounted has become another Catatonia legend. They had arrived back in Cardiff from a record company sponsored party and there was nowhere to go. Cerys invited everyone back to her house. In the front room was a sixties cocktail bar with a light on it, along with a television and a few other items. Having made her mind up that the telly was in the way, she decided to rearrange the furniture and, in a strange twist on the usual rock-star-in-hotel story, promptly threw her own TV out of her own window.

"I'm fine when I'm sober," she admitted, "but when I get a couple of drinks down me anything seems possible. The TV was only a shitty one anyway, a black and white portable that someone won at Bingo and gave me. It all made sense."

Chez Cerys at this time was a rented house in Cardiff. There was a bench press with a heavily padded deck against the wall; home-made soft furnishings; the obligatory stash of traffic signs and council collectibles, a painting of a Welsh lady complete with tall hat; and newspaper and magazine pictures of Manchester United players on the walls. Against one wall was the bar in the form of the prow of a boat on which the now departed telly used to perch.

Lloyd Grossman would have had a field day. "Who lives in a house like this?"

Owen maintains that a lot of things that get attributed to Cerys, have actually been done by other band members. "From the outset, people are just looking for a peg to hang you on." Crazy, Welsh, drinking monsters seemed to be Catatonia's title elect. In fact it was Owen who got the band chucked out of Stringfellows in London.

They were at a Romo party, trying to become Romos, getting into some make-up and that, when Owen tried to nick a bottle of tequila. They were all grabbed by the necks and ejected. (As an underage music fan, I used to go a club run by Mr Stringfellow and his brother in Sheffield in the 60s – *The Mojo* – it was a great live music club, well ahead of its time.)

So in addition to establishing a growing reputation for their music and gigs, the band's notoriety for rabble rousing soon meant they were becoming the darlings of the music media. They were also creating hard work for any future biographer of the band, who would have to try and find out which stories were factual and which were contrived for publicity.

When they did manage to grab some spare time in between recording and touring, it allowed Cerys to indulge in one of her passions at her Cardiff home – gardening.

It was to become a solitary yet fulfilling hobby for her, whether it be caring for her collection of Japanese plants or tending to her vegetables and herbs in her small back garden, or aspiring to grow a championship marrow. (In 1999, she would be photographed in her garden, wearing an agricultural smock. These photographs were to form part of a collection which went on display at the National Museum and Gallery in Cardiff.)

This brief period of relaxation came shortly before Catatonia returned to the Phoenix Festival, an event eagerly anticipated by the singer who, in her own words, wanted "to blow everyone away this year". Instead, "I'd been doing my usual, had a few drinks beforehand," she explains, "singing my lungs off, not a care in the world, cool as I could be and I fell over a monitor. What the fuck? Who put that monitor there? It was the worst. But it was quite funny. I got up and carried on."

A lot of bands who appeared at the festival were featured on a compilation disc, appropriately titled *The Phoenix Album*. Catatonia's contribution was the live version of "Way Beyond Blue" from the Mark Radcliffe session.

After Phoenix, there were festivals in Spain and France, which would give Cerys the chance to brush up on her linguistic skills. She claims to speak Spanish very badly, and evidence of this would appear on "Acapulco Gold," which has some Spanish lyrics – but a Spanish fan told them they referred to the sun as 'el soleil' when it is actually 'el sol'.

One country they had yet to play was Japan, but in July a mini-album was released there entitled *Tourist*. This contained the following tracks; "Sweet Catatonia", "Lost Cat", "All Girls Are Fly", "Indigo Blind", "Acapulco Gold", "Tourist", "To And Fro", "Sweet Catatonia" (Live - Mark Radcliffe session), "Whale" (Live – Mark Radcliffe acoustic session) and "Cut You Inside". It was mainly material that they had been playing at gigs. This album is now very difficult to get hold of, even as an import.

The summer festival circuit was punctuated by several appearances on the *Radio 1 Roadshow* but there was a bit of a problem developing between Catatonia and the US outfit Rocket From The Crypt.

It arose during a relaxed interview as the band sat around with a journalist. The chat got around to drinking in hotel bars, and they mentioned that they had spent a lot of time in the same hotels as Rocket From The Crypt. This prompted Owen to say, "They're not rock 'n' roll, they're just a bunch of pussies."

This led to bad feeling on both sides with threats being made in all directions. Owen explained, "Now isn't it obvious when you say something like that about a gang of eight guys from San Diego, who look the way they do, that I wasn't being totally serious?" The situation simmered for a while before it calmed down without any recriminations.

On August 20th, Catatonia played once again at The Monarch in Camden Town, London. No big deal, except that I was supposed to be attending. One of my neighbours was having a domestic problem and asked if I would watch her house and keep an eye on her children while she got it sorted. By the time she came back it was too late for me to go.

On a positive note, it was a sign that I was making some progress if people were asking me to help them. The "black holes" which had plagued me were becoming much less frequent but other symptoms persisted. There were times when I became incredibly tired for no reason at all. I once fell asleep standing up, leaning on my spade whilst digging my vegetable patch.

I would sometimes go to shops and either ask for things they obviously did not sell, such as potatoes from the chemist, or even forget completely what I had gone for. I regularly asked the bus driver for a pint of bitter instead of a 50p ticket. Some days my memory was crystal clear, on others I could not remember my date of birth.

I had just enjoyed a short period of reasonable health and was keen to go up to London and take in that gig, but compensation awaited that weekend.

At the Reading festival on Saturday August 24th, Cerys displayed her latest pop wardrobe accessories – red boxing gloves (which she thought were "dead sexy") – and promptly offered to fight anyone who wanted to take her on. She admitted to liking boxing "for the violence" and was feeling aggressive, even to the extent of threatening to take the place of the freshly retired Chris Eubank. No wonder Rocket From The Crypt kept their distance.

The band were displaying greater confidence on stage and were relishing the busy schedule, especially the outdoor gigs – one of which, the Eisteddfod, took place in their home country, with Catatonia playing on the Saturday.

At this Eisteddfod, the Super Furry Animals were frowned upon for singing in English. Cerys took a dim view of this dissent, and thought those people who say Welsh bands should only sing in Welsh were prats.

The heavy schedule of gigs had them touring with better-fancied bands such as Puressence, Marion and Salad. In certain music quarters they were being described as a cult band which pleased them because they considered it gave a debonair quality to what they were trying to do.

Critics were making assessments of the band and drawing comparisons with other outfits, generally with Sleeper, who were being touted as the band for the future. The music industry was getting used to the idea of bands that were her (lead singer) and them (the rest of the band).

Paul was not impressed with this and pointed out that they had resisted attempts to be like that. Here were five individuals who contributed different things to the band, each with their own strengths and weaknesses.

There was no big boss or cowering band members. The singer is going to be the one at the front and that's the way it should be. No one had any problem with that.

Cerys had accepted from the outset, that, when she sang with Mark, it was to allow him to take a back seat. "They love it. They're laughing all the way. I'm their bloody workhorse, but it's a role I relish. I love it. They take the piss out of me all the time and they revel in the freedom they have. You can always get someone to go out in front and dress in funny clothes and sing and dance about a bit."

On Monday August 26th, a song that was to become a favourite at any Catatonia gig was released – "You've Got A Lot To Answer For". On CD1 the B-sides were "Do You Believe In Me" and "Dimbran", on CD2 "You Can" and "All Girls Are Fly" (Da-De? Remix). A cassette was also released with B-sides "Do You Believe In Me" and "Blow The Millennium Blow" (Splott Remix) – Splott being a district of Cardiff.

"Do You Believe In Me" was the first song released that was not listed as a Matthews/Roberts composition, instead the name Paul Jones joined Mark and Cerys as one of the co-writers. This proved to be too much of a shock for some people, because a label was affixed to promotional copies of the CD, proclaiming that "Do You Believe In Me" was co-written with the Welsh crooner himself, Tom Jones".

Catatonia now appealed to national radio presenters such as Mark Radcliffe of Radio 1, who threatened to bare his bum in a Spud-U-Like if the single wasn't a hit. Also, the first public performance of "You've Got A Lot To Answer For" took place at the London Hippodrome when the group was featured on Radio 1's *Evening Session*.

The record gave the band their first reasonable public exposure via extensive radio play, TV use of the tune and an extensive tour. Cerys herself rated it as a "simple, lovely song". The record charted at number 35 for one week and then dropped out. Spud-U-Like customers at least were overjoyed with this brief Top 40 showing as they would not be presented with Mark Radcliffe's arse for use as a toast rack.

Critical acclaim was forthcoming from the music media. *New Musical Express* described "You've Got A Lot To Answer For" as "a ten-storey love song with a killer twist, sonorous church bell guitars and a towering Alpine tune."

According to the same paper, Mark came up with the idea for the song while waiting in the queue at the local Spar supermarket in Cardiff. A few of his friends had become fathers but had decided not to move in with the mothers of their kids. Consequently, they were getting hounded by the Child Support Agency.

Single mothers from South Wales had been a favourite target for Tory politicians who claimed that teenage Welsh girls were abusing the welfare system by taking their biology practical a little too seriously. The song echoes the sentiments of Mark and Cerys about this issue.

"You've Got A Lot To Answer For" is a highlight at Catatonia gigs. As soon as Cerys announces onstage, "This is for you lot," everyone knows what's coming. Three minutes of jumping up and down – whatever your age – crowd surfing, fans putting arms around each other, exchanging sweat as the linked human chains sway side to side, front to back. It is a magical moment and has caused some of the younger fans to show concern about my health. "You'll have a heart attack, doing that at your age," they say. "If ever you get to reach my age and you find me still doing it at a Catatonia gig, then start worrying," is my reply.

Since they first included the song in their set, I cannot remember it ever being omitted. I do, however, possess a set list for the band's proposed appearance at Glastonbury on June 28th 1997. For some reason, "YGAL-TAF" was missing – no gig either, venue flooded.

The B-side "Do You Believe In Me," was to be ranked number 6 in a top ten of drug-related songs by *Select* magazine in August 1999 for its lyrics, *"I'm Andy Cole's tortured soul/ lost out again in front of goal/ I wish I had your cocaine confidence."*

In a conversation with Mark, he once told me he thought Manchester United should sell Andy Cole. I thought, "That's not being grateful after the money you've made out of that song." After all, it would have been a bugger if he was trying to rhyme it with Ole Gunnar Solskjaer.

September 10th saw Catatonia once again perform at the *In The City* festival, this time at the Temple Bar Music Centre in Dublin. There was something doomed about this event for Catatonia, but they were determined to be sharp to make up for the previous year's debacle.

Pre-festival, however, things did not go smoothly – a portent of what was to come. Firstly, there was a laborious journey in the van from Cardiff to Holyhead enlivened by hours of smoking joints, listening to techno and old 60s CDs and watching a comedy video of Kevin McAtear. On arrival at Holyhead, they found that the ferry had gone without them, so their reward was a miserable overnight stay.

Eventually the band arrived at the venue and when they appeared on stage, looked designer-casual and impressive. Cerys as usual was up for it.

She shadowboxed and wowed the audience with her precocious smile. The start of the gig augered well, but into the set they started to suffer sound problems. Cerys remained enthusiastic and did all she could to retain the support of the crowd, but she finally had to admit they'd lost it.

After the show the band locked their dressing room door and remained inside for a good thirty minutes, presumably holding a post-mortem. On emerging all was well again as they set about seeking refreshments and a party.

Shortly after, on September 13th at the Botanique Festival La Rotonde in Brussels, they made amends with a gutsy live performance. The band had now acquired a staunch following. "They tend to have moustaches though," commented Owen. "It's a bit worrying. We seem to be attracting lots of mustachios. Especially the girls."

By now Owen had been given the nickname "Worry Beads" by the crew (he admits to worrying for a living) whilst Cerys reveled in her new label of Queenie. She was also teased about young boy groupies. She responded by saying she would more likely be tempted by male groupies aged 35 to 45. (Counts me out, for one.)

Amidst all the touring in 1996, Mark had noticed an unusual co-inci-dence that kept appearing in the press. In every town the band played, they were reports of a flasher at work. The in-group humour was directed towards Paul being the guilty party as he had developed a nervous habit of having to go out for a walk before gigs. Cerys herself was flashed near the Columbia Hotel in London. She reacted by shouting "pervert" along with a few well-chosen phrases of anglo-saxon origin, only for a passing family to promptly complain about her choice of language.

Eventually, after taking time out during the tours, Catatonia gave the fans something that they had been waiting for – their first album. Entitled *Way Beyond Blue*, it was released on September 30th. It contained "Lost Cat", "Sweet Catatonia", "Some Half Baked Ideal Called Wonderful", "You've Got A Lot To Answer For", "Infantile", "Dream On", "Bleed", "This Boy Can't Swim", "Painful", "Whale", "For Tinkerbell", "Way Beyond Blue" and the obligatory hidden track "Gyda Gwen". It was pretty much a studio version of their set list and covered material they had been performing for two and a half years. Ironically, only "Infantile" and "Way Beyond Blue" had not been released in some form or other before.

Geoff Travis had put Stephen Street (who had worked with The Smiths, Blur and The Cranberries) in charge of production sessions with co-pro-ducer Paul Sampson, while mixes were done by Julia Mendelsohn and

Tommy D, (who had also produced the Sugarcubes, A Tribe Called Quest and The Shamen.) The album which started out being recorded in London (Maison Rouge) was added to in several studios in Cornwall, North Wales, South Wales, Surrey, and Coventry as the band toured the country.

Way Beyond Blue showed that the group was much more than just a guitar band, utilising a wide range of instrumentation without necessarily worrying about how to play the material live. As with any group of five individuals, rows and arguments developed but eventually they came together to make sure the right songs went on the album.

Time Out claimed it was a "supreme debut" but Stephen Dalton in *New Musical Express* excelled himself. He referred to the band as "Knackered old bastards with dodgy pub-rock roots," before acknowledging that "they are still doing it better than the rest." He professed that they were not "patronising the New Welsh Wave tag and had produced an album of archetypal rock themes, handled with passion, imagination and a heroic disregard for fashion."

"Bleed" in particular was described as, "a three-minute-punk-pop blast-erama featuring a top muso key change and a heart-stopping precipice, where the music falls away to leave Cerys pedaling in mid-air like that mental coyote in *Roadrunner* cartoons." He summed the tunes up as "big-hearted, lived-in, lusty, boozy, heartbroken and ready for a fight – or a shag – at all times." A description that also could have been applied to the band themselves. Dalton concluded that *Way Beyond Blue* was "a tremendously assured debut." A couple of years after its release, *Melody Maker* commented that *Way Beyond Blue* was "charming and uplifting but most of all, criminally underrated."

Certainly at the time, the album failed to make a significant impact reaching a highest chart position of 40, partly due to distribution problems and the fact that many of the fans already owned most of the songs. However, a fair cross section of the Catatonia audience still rate this as their favourite Catatonia album.

In retrospect, Paul and Mark reflected that the album may have fared better had it been released somewhat earlier, around Christmas 1995. Owen, while remaining very proud of *Way Beyond Blue*, conceded that they had not been ambitious enough and that the album was quite narrow in terms of their capabilities.

Cerys remains philosophical about this period in the band's history. Pop music is a very competitive environment and she wanted her band to be the best. She had had great hopes for *Way Beyond Blue* just as she had had great hopes from the first moment she picked up the guitar.

The Welsh Nationalist movement has benefited from the success of Welsh bands, but Catatonia demonstrated their unwillingness to pay lip service to this by including the Welsh language track "Gyda Gwen" only as a hidden track on the album. Cerys refused to discuss this at the time "because it's supposed to be a surprise for the punters." Mark however, insisted that it was for all those nationalists who listen to the album and thought the band had sold out because the track listing shows only English songs.

I was on the telephone at home in Sheffield when I heard some muffled talking (which starts off the track), I put the phone down and went to the door thinking someone was trying to get in. I had forgotten all about the CD. I went back to the phone and told my friend, "I can't understand this, there's some Welsh wanker jabbering away somewhere in here and I can't see anybody. I must be pissed!"

Cue music and song and the penny drops. Apologies to Cerys.

* * *

Life gives no guarantee of happiness and sweetness has a habit of turning sour. A relationship breaking down is never pleasant and it can often prove bitter and stressful. If it happens within a working environment then it can cause problems for colleagues as well as the individuals concerned, creating a strained atmosphere. Mark and Cerys' relationship was ending around this time. Things had not been going well between them for a while and Mark decided things had run their course and moved out of the house they were sharing.

Shortly after he started a relationship with another girl and they are still an item to this day. Cerys freely admitted that the split was difficult and influenced the dynamics of the band. There were moments when it became very awkward to continue, but they managed to pull through. She claims that if they talk about things at all now, then they talk about it in the songs, which accounts for a lot of the lyrics being bittersweet. The close songwriting collaboration effectively ended with the relationship – there is a distinct difference between the songs written before and after the split. Many found it sad that they would no longer write songs in the vein of their earlier material, but it does not mean the quality of the output has been affected, rather more a change in spirit and direction.

It has been chronicled that some fans were not aware of Mark and Cerys' relationship until they split up. Certainly, up to this period in their career they had chosen not to give many interviews, so presumably a lot of music journos were not aware of this aspect of their personal lives. But most fans of my acquaintance were certainly in the know.

To date, it is Cerys' longest relationship. The fact that she can still get very upset when interviewers bring the matter up is a sure indication of the internal torment she suffered privately. Even now, her and Mark being in the same room together can occasionally cause problems.

Cerys does not like talking about the man who broke her heart in that particular context. She'd rather leave it in the past, but Mark seems able to ride it out in his own way. Each person has their own method of coping with situations. He does not find it hurtful or painful being in the same band as an ex-girlfriend. "To be honest, I think it's embarrassing when band members copulate with each other," he adds. "It's ungainly... We're much better off since we've split actually."

From a more personal viewpoint however, I have seen several instances where Mark is still protective of Cerys. Like most relationships, they enjoyed happy times and endured sadness. Some unions create children who are treasured by the partners, Mark and Cerys gave birth to Catatonia. It is to their credit, that they both loved the music of Catatonia too much to let their personal feelings change or break up the band.

Cerys reflected in 1999 that, "the last album (*International Velvet*) worked, because it was getting more and more difficult to stay together, so we had a lot at stake – more and more to put in to make it a better record. We just poured it into the music. And when we're on stage it has to mean something to put up with that shit [emotional stress]. If it hurt that much to carry on in the band, and it did hurt a lot, then when you actually get on stage, or when you put something down on record, then it actually meant something, because you put an awful lot of effort into doing it."

Catatonia's ability to sweat blood for their cause probably helped them keep the momentum going and ease their problems. In any event, a heavy touring schedule was going to keep them busy. A fifteen-gig tour was lined up supporting the Manic Street Preachers, starting at the Forum in Livingston on October 5th, to be swiftly followed by a headlining thirteen-gig tour to promote *Way Beyond Blue* taking them to their final gig at the Stage in Hanley on November 12th.

When following a band on tour – apart from the fact that your friends dismiss you as a lunatic – it is logical to assume that that the tour will follow a sequence. Play a gig, next town along the road, play a gig next town along the road, etc. This is seldom the case. The October tour, for

example, went; 14th Sheffield, 15th Blackburn, 17th Hull, 18th Carlisle –
hardly the AA prescribed route! On a positive note, it helped my battle
with depression and the bottle. By 1996, there was hardly any time for me
to get paralytic.

Despite a general overhaul and upgrading of their musical equipment in
keeping with their new financial security, they still suffered at some venues
with dodgy acoustics and decrepit PA systems. How easy it is to dismiss
any band on a one-off gig at a venue not equipped for their musical presentation.

Cerys confessed that she had previously been of the opinion that they
were terrible. Often, she would end up shouting into the microphone
because she could not hear the rest of the band. Now she noticed a significant improvement in their abilities, and as a result her ambitions expanded
to wanting to play Australia or sample the sushi in Japan.

The band's musical horizons were also beginning to open up. They were
still determined to try out new songs in the studio whenever they got the
opportunity. Mark was keen to work on some ideas that they had formu-
lated, and there were plans for more adventurous material that would be a
departure from what they had produced so far. As a result, they favoured
a different approach to their musical arrangement.

Far from sitting back and playing to the old tried and tested formula
as so many acts have done, they decided to test the theory that "fortune
favours the brave".

Music is a great healer, leveller and communicator. There are times, in
certain communities, where it is also a source of comfort and thanksgiving.
Welsh boxer, Johnny Owen, tragically died after being injured in a boxing
match. He was a highly regarded fighter and a much-loved person. Fierce
Panda and Townhill Records produced a CD and double LP entitled *Dial
M For Merthyr* as a tribute to him. Most of the locally or nationally famous
Welsh bands offered tracks. Catatonia contributed "To and Fro." It is a
beautiful album that displayed the full kaleidoscope of Welsh music at the
time.

More people were now getting curious about Catatonia. The state I was
in, I was losing lady friends as quickly as I acquired them – and I used
to buy *Loaded* (a lads' magazine) I'll be honest, for the reasons it was published. To my surprise in one particular issue I chanced upon an interview
and photo of Cerys. Firstly, I'd never read that far before and had not
realised there was a music section. Secondly, there was Cerys holding a
lager bottle – whatever next.

She was asked what it was like to be the only girl in the band. She sighed and said it can be impossibly difficult. "They get these moods on them every so often and they spend all their time reading their fashion magazines and talking about clothes. And you're always having to stop the van so they can do their make-up."

The usual incidents were dragged out, but at the end of the interview, Cerys asked in a mocking tone, "Will you be needing me to get my tits out? None of you *Loaded* readers can read, can you?" she giggled. If she did, the photos were not printed!

On November 18th, "Bleed" was re-released in a 2 CD format. CD1 featured "Bleed", "Way Beyond Blue" (Acoustic Session, Phoenix), "Painful!" (Live – Reading Festival 1FM) whilst CD2 had "Bleed" (Version 2), "Do You Believe In Me" (Reading Festival), "Bleed" (Live – Evening Session). There was a cassette released featuring "Bleed", "Way Beyond Blue", (Acoustic Session Phoenix), "Bleed" (Live – Evening Session). A 7" vinyl was also issued featuring "Bleed" and "Bleed" (Live – Evening Session).

This time the record reached a highest chart entry of 46. It possibly wasn't helped by the fact that the word "bullshit" features in the lyrics and when the band performed the song on TV the word had to be edited out. This also applied to the official promo disc.

As if to confirm the nature of the year for Catatonia, *Volume 17* included the band singing "Mickey" (aka "Some Half Baked Ideal Called Wonderful") in its compilation which was released around the Christmas holiday period. Mark explained that the song was written about a paranoid bloke who lived downstairs from him. The guy had heard the song, but as he was always pissed he could make no sense of it.

I was getting a good collection of Catatonia recordings. Every night from mid-1995 onwards, I would put one of their tapes into my Walkman and go to sleep listening to them. It played a major therapeutic part in overcoming my sleeping problems. I further sensed I was making progress when I started listening to the rest of my record collection during the good days.

The only times I still had difficulty sleeping was following one of the band's concerts. I get such a tremendous adrenaline surge after a gig that I often go three days without sleep or even feeling tired. It is the cheapest buzz I can get.

For its Christmas 1996 issue, *New Musical Express* ran a feature which involved taking Cerys, Julie from Tiger, Debbie from Echobelly, Marie from Kenicke and *NME* journalist Johnny Cigarettes on a drinking session round Camden, ostensibly playing pub golf.

The results were hilarious. Highlights included Debbie fondling Cerys' tits in a pub doorway and Cerys laying on the floor, screaming how good she was in bed. Everyone generally got completely pissed and made complete idiots of themselves, all in the name of "pub golf". "It was mostly girls," Cerys explains "and it was really good fun."

It was to become a pilgrimage for me to see Catatonia in Wales, and in particular in Cardiff in December. Most groups would have cried off the punishing schedules that Catatonia were still undertaking. December saw them on a four-gig tour supporting Shed Seven, with a performance at Cardiff Arena in the middle, where they and the Super Furry Animals supported the Manic Street Preachers.

Despite the abundance of live work, there was still no tangible advancement in terms of a breakthrough in selling records. Catatonia's live performances were selling them as a band, but the ultimate goal seemed as far away as ever.

Perhaps the lack of time to write caused by constant touring had temporarily stifled their creativity. Over the previous twelve months, when it seemed they must surely make a significant impression on the British pop charts, major success had consistently eluded them. Despite my faith in the band, I was not alone in wondering if they would ever make it after coming so close.

This optimism I had in the band was slowly percolating into me as well, although bouts of depression still affected me. I had taken in more open-air gigs during the year and I felt comfortable to be close to the band. I could not get my head round being anywhere near to them indoors. Whilst I was sure my condition was improving, I was aware that it would be gradual, if I was to return to the person I once was. I was totally determined to hang onto my lifeline.

I would get some good days and some that had me trying to run up the wall. I never knew when these would occur, there was no advance warning, but for the moment Catatonia, Wales and music were providing the desired therapy. The answer to my problems was staring me in the face and yet I still couldn't see it.

For some time I had been subject to ridicule at home as a result of my following an "unknown" Welsh band. Perhaps I was suffering the first signs of senile dementia. As usual I offered to put my money where my mouth was. On December 31st 1996, before I got pissed to welcome the New

Year in, I offered anybody, any money, to disprove that Cerys Matthews was rapidly becoming Britain's finest female pop singer/songwriter/stage performer and that Catatonia would hit the big time in the not too distant future. There were no takers.

YOU MAKE IT GREAT
MAKE IT A BRILLIANT THING

"Music's always been there, the answer to any question asked. That's as corny as fuck, but it's the truth."

Cerys Matthews

By the mid-1990s dance music had taken off and DJ sets were replacing bands in many clubs and venues. There were several quality groups, Catatonia included, knocking on the door of success but nobody seemed prepared to answer. It was becoming apparent that it would require something special if one of these bands was going to break through.

In camp Catatonia, after the touring and recording workload of 1996, the band took time out from the UK public in January and February 1997. Their first appearances of the year were scheduled to be abroad, with gigs planned for the Paradiso, Amsterdam on February 14th, New York Brownies on March 11th supporting the Boo Radleys, The South by Southwest Festival in Austin, Texas on March 14th and the Los Angeles Viper Room on March 17th. These gigs were to be followed by playing the Greece Rodon Club in Athens, supporting Gene on March 29th.

Valentines night in Amsterdam, at the London Calling festival, saw sets from both Catatonia and the Stereophonics. Both bands went down well and in addition to a deserved ovation from the audience, Cerys received a Valentine card from Kelly Jones of the Stereophonics.

"I drew this face thing on a Valentine card," said Kelly, "and gave it to Swampy, our drum tech, to pass on to her."

In Amsterdam, Cerys' grasp of the local lingo gave her an opportunity to widen the education of the boys by teaching them a few phrases. Ever keen to play the practical joke, it wasn't long before the sound of four Welsh blokes addressing people with "Hello handsome" in Dutch turned a few heads.

Catatonia seemed to have re-charged their batteries from the efforts of the previous year and following the Dutch gig they were clearly relishing the opportunity to impress the Americans.

Michael Krugman of *Raygun* magazine conducted a brief interview with Cerys after the band played Austin, Texas.

"You're the cunt what was singing along," she said. "How d'you know the words?"

"Well," he replied, "I bought the singles."

"Didja? Cheers!" replied Cerys.

Another interview successfully concluded, then it was off to Los Angeles. They shared a plane with Ray Charles, the drummer from Guns 'n' Roses and Sally Field.

Ensconced in their Hollywood hotel, Cerys managed to put some colour into the proceedings. Posing in the jacuzzi, she had forgotten that her hair had been bleached. When she visited the bathroom, she discovered her hair had turned green. It brought back memories of her fancy dress outing as a mountain. Fortunately, on this occasion, there were no fashion accessories such as sheep on her thighs.

America wasn't without its irritations during the short tour. They were not impressed with the Viper Room in LA, where punters were not allowed to sit on the floor or lean on the walls without getting hassle from the bouncers.

Compensation awaited though as Status Quo moved into the same hotel in LA, which pleased Cerys, "So, it was all a bit mad. I had to get their autographs for my housemates!"

Catatonia duly performed their gigs in LA and New York State and were well received. Paul and Owen agreed afterwards that there is a long held obsession with breaking America, but that America had more or less broken them. Paul concluded that the Americans "had the biggest car parks in the world." Cerys, meanwhile, was still musing over why Uncle Sam had never heard of the Wombles. "I can't respect any country that doesn't know who Uncle Bulgaria is."

On returning from the USA, Cerys discovered that her voice had become croaky so she went for a check-up at the doctors. With the aid of a microscopic camera it was diagnosed that she had been straining her vocal cords too much. It was obvious that she had to rest them and as a result the Athens gig had to be cancelled.

As well as strained vocal cords, Cerys had acquired an ant farm in the USA. The break gave her a chance to spend a whole day digging in her back garden for ants to put in it. An experience she found, "very therapeutic, watching them crawl around." Handling her little charges, however, proved problematic. "When I pick them up I sometimes accidentally pull their legs off. Do they grow spare legs like spiders?" she wondered.

With a forthcoming tour looming, her idea was to put them in the fridge, but her flatmates soon put a damper on this plan as being unhygienic.

While Cerys was pondering the limb regeneration properties of insects, *Twin Town*, the movie, set in and around Swansea, opened on April 11th (Cerys birthday appropriately enough). *Twin Town* offered many character parts, which were gratefully accepted by Welsh actors and actresses. In addition the film boasted an excellent soundtrack featuring the cream of the crop of current Welsh bands, including "You've Got A Lot To Answer For". The album was released ahead of the film on April 7th.

After the enforced rest, Cerys' throat was now fully recovered and there was a short (by Catatonia's standards) ten-gig tour of the UK starting at The Room in Hull on April 13th and finishing at The Waterfront, Norwich on April 24th. Originally the tour was to promote their new single "Mulder and Scully" scheduled for release on May 12th, 1997, but the single was withheld, for what turned out to be eight months. Asked to comment on the deferred release, Cerys explained, "We had a single called "A Case For Mulder And Scully – The Ex-Files", but the record company didn't want to release it until the album comes out. Erm, I think Bugs Bunny [Warner's] has run out of money."

The gigs did, however, provide them with an opportunity to try out a set of new songs.

While "Mulder and Scully" made a huge impact when it was finally released, the delay was puzzling to onlookers. Was there some marketing strategy that was not obviously apparent? It was no secret that Warners were close to dropping the band, so was this a cost-limitation ploy? After all they had signed the band presumably to make records, or was I missing something?

On this tour, I managed to see Catatonia at the Sheffield Leadmill, Manchester's Hop 'n' Grape, Gloucester Guildhall, Liverpool Lomax and Newcastle Riverside. There was a different sort of buzz to these gigs than others I had witnessed. It was like standing back from a lit firework that was taking its time to explode into full glory. As for me, I still went diving for cover if any member of the band came anywhere near me, but I was more confident now than for sometime. "Jump Or Be Sane," was never more relevant.

At last I was back in a position of feeling more optimistic about life. I despised the person that I had become in 1993, but I knew full well that I had been powerless to stop my decline. Equally, I knew that if I slipped back, then that would be the end. I could not go through that again.

At the end of April I suffered what was to be the last of my "black holes". Obviously, I did not know this at the time. I was determined to come back fighting. Fighting for what, I had not decided. Whenever I hear "Do You Believe In Me?" I try to fight back the tears, often unsuccessfully, as I mentally thank those who did believe in me – when the arsehole writing this book did not.

In early May, the band was back across the Atlantic for three gigs in Canada, supporting Suede at The Warehouse in Toronto, Barrymore's in Ottawa and The Metropolis, Montreal. Time to enjoy the scenery was non-existent because they had to return immediately to Wales for a hometown event. On May 11th, the Big Noise Festival was held in Cardiff Bay to celebrate the centenary of the world's first radio broadcast.

In an interview backstage, Cerys talked about playing a gig in Cardiff and again showed her domesticity. "It's quite nice, just to have five minutes, you know, to come here and be home all day and do my washing. I put some out today and it got rained on, but it doesn't matter, does it really?" (I am sure Madonna does exactly the same thing.)

Catatonia put on an outstanding show, although most people recall the inebriated invasion of Space's set by a very wobbly Cerys. Blame it on the washing powder – it doesn't mix with strong lager.

The festival though was different to most, and prompted Owen to comment, "That was a weird gig. The crowd were 25 yards away from you before you'd even started and in between songs you couldn't hear people clapping or whatever, all you could hear was just the hum of your amp behind you."

For Glastonbury 1997 I acquired a luxury tent which unwittingly gained an indoor and outdoor swimming pool and a waterbed. There is something special about the outdoor festivals that I attend – torrential rain. When people who know me find out I am going to a festival they cancel their booking and go to the dentist instead. When Catatonia played in the tent at the Phoenix festival, guess who was under the section that leaked?

On June 28th, Catatonia arrived at "Glasto" and managed to get their gear out of the van and as far as the stage, only to be told that their spot and those of the Sneaker Pimps and Kenicke had been cancelled, because "the electrics were knackered".

"We went down," Cerys confirmed, "but the stage sank and we couldn't play. I got as far as swapping toilet roll with John Squire in the backstage toilets. We were totally gutted 'cos I'd had a wager with Mark. He doesn't like doing festivals so he bet me we wouldn't play, so I lost. We didn't stick around because I had my stilettos on, and they probably weren't the right footwear to have."

So it was a mud-splattered band that had to load up the van and go back to the studio. Owen in particular was very disappointed, because this festival means so much to him. Having spent his holidays attending Glastonbury every year as a punter, it had become his ambition to take to the stage there.

Catatonia took most of the other festivals by storm that year. Steve Lamacq, rated their performance at the Phoenix Festival as, "one of the best acts on," whilst their set at T-in-the-Park, "was exceptional". Lamacq championed the Catatonia cause and had become a good friend of the band.

By this time they rarely played a bad gig. It gave me the opportunity to reflect on some of the shambolic performances I had witnessed, the miles I had covered and the money I had spent. There have never been any regrets from me. If anything, it is far more fulfilling seeing a group go through the mill, learning the hard way, dropping more bollocks than a serial castrator.

I would be lying if I said I had seen Cerys change from a lady who calls a 'spade' a 'fucking shovel' into a choirgirl, but while she may have slightly moderated her language during a set, her stage presence was rapidly developing. Cerys now seemed to combine the cool, sexy, cocksure self-assurance of Debbie Harry with the zany, mischievousness of Cyndi Lauper.

As the stage act was getting more polished, so people were now noticing the singer more than ever as she threw everything into the act, occasionally revealing more than her vocal skills.

"Look Ceh, onstage, just shut your legs a bit", a very good friend offered as advice, prompting the reply, "But I can't sing with my legs closed. It's impossible. Shirley Bassey's voice coach says you've got to open your airways. I got it wrong. I took it the wrong way."

The next major gig was the Reading Festival on Friday, August 22nd. While on stage a giant balloon passed by Cerys, whose eyes lit up.

"I want to meet the man who that condom belongs to," she said, grinning.

Owen also had cause to grin. Virgin Radio had given each artist a special card that entitled them to a certain number of free drinks – the card being marked by the bar staff. He quickly discovered that his shirt was made of a fibre that could rub the mark off, and consequently far exceeded his ten-drink quota that night.

Not all of the outdoor gigs were the mainline festivals however. When a gig scheduled for Swansea Airport on August 8th, comprising of Welsh bands including Catatonia, was cancelled, a replacement gig was organised by the Swansea Rotary Club. Catatonia were given a support slot to Terror-vision and Chumbawamba at the city's Singleton Park on Bank Holiday Monday, August 25th.

Having come all the way back to Swansea, Catatonia were disappointed when they were dispatched to a little side stage with no PA. "That was a load of shit really," Cerys explained. "Especially as it was home town-ish and it was the first time all my family and friends had come to see us. Some had never seen us play before. It just sounded like crap."

On Thursday September 18th *Melody Maker* interviewed Catatonia under the headline "The Hit Man and Her" about "I Am The Mob" which was to be the band's next single. It took place at the Grosvenor Casino, Cardiff. Mark and Cerys were playfully quizzed about the lyrics to the song, and whether there was a mobster side to the band. Drinks were never far from hand.

After the interview, Cerys rose to rapturous applause, took a seat, grabbed a beer, and yapped away with one of her friends. The *Melody Maker* interviewer was struck by the incident enough to comment, "Surely they don't have time to have regular lives on top of being celebs?"

"We do," asserted Cerys.

The fun and games for the evening were not yet over as this was the night of the devolution vote in Wales. Catatonia had all supported the "Yes" campaign and Cerys had been sporting a "Yes for Wales" T-shirt for some time. So, as a highly vociferous supporter of the "Yes" campaign, she had been invited to take part in a pundit's round table for the BBC, supposedly representing 'Young Hip Wales'.

Prior to the discussion, which went on air at 1.00am, Cerys had enjoyed a lengthy excursion round the hospitality bar, in addition to the liquor she had consumed at the interview earlier. As the debate accelerated near to 4.00am, Cerys put forward her one and only question. She asked very loudly in Welsh, "Who's Sian Lloyd fucking?"

All this was done for a £10 bet, which she won, but Cerys found herself excluded from discussions. The incident nevertheless caused quite a fuss. The peeved weather girl turned pro-Welsh Assembly campaigner then drafted a defamation of character writ, only to reconsider, when it was pointed out to her that the youth vote was integral to winning the referendum.

"There was a flurry of legal letters," explained Cerys, "and then she issued a statement saying she liked our last album and listened to it all the time in the car."

"They're not allowed within ten miles of each other," chuckles Mark.

"Afterwards, I got a nice letter from the Head of S4C," she explains, "which read, 'Dear Cerys, you are no longer welcome on Welsh television, particularly live shows. I have forthwith mentioned to my producer that you are not welcome to do live shows.' And I'm the biggest talent in Wales."

Cerys remained unrepentant. After all it gave the band its best publicity for quite some time.

Although Catatonia had so far failed to break through, one song which really paved the way was "I Am The Mob". This was the first release from what was to be the album *International Velvet*. It went on sale on October 6th, which seemed to contradict the opinion that "Mulder and Scully" was shelved because the album was not ready.

It was released in CD form, cassette and 7" vinyl (the band like to release their material on 7" vinyl, because of its collectable nature, but big record labels are reluctant to do so. In fact the album *Way Beyond Blue* was issued on vinyl and deleted almost as soon as it came out). B-sides on the CD were "Jump Or Be Sane", "My Selfish Gene" and "I Am The Mob" (Luca Bras mix). It reached a chart high of number 40. Once again, the song wowed the critics but failed to sell, despite the release being neatly timed to coincide with the 25th anniversary of Francis Ford Coppola's film *The Godfather*.

Sales were not helped when BBC Radio 1 decreed that it should not be played during the day time. There appeared to be a problem with the suitability of the lyrics. When it comes to double standards, however, England are world champions. While Catatonia faced a ban, "Smack My Bitch Up" by the Prodigy was allowed full air play. Perhaps the BBC thought this was a gentle English ballad, or an excerpt from the Glyndebourne Festival – bodily assault section.

"I Am the Mob" starts off with a sound sample taken from *Jenny Jones,* a typical American confrontational TV programme. The band was watching the programme while they were at Monnow Valley studios taking a break from recording. During the snippett a girl comes face to face with a girl who has bullied her at school. Eventually she plucks up courage and explodes in a fury, saying to her tormentor, "How would you feel if someone came along and beat the living daylights out of you?"

It is not a song about the Mafia films, as the band went to great lengths to explain, but more a way of expressing the frustration and anger that they had felt over the last year. Despite its low chart entry, it has become synonymous with Catatonia and has become a live favourite.

Not many record companies release a single so far ahead of an album, when a song has so much potential. Was Blanco Y Negro thinking that *International Velvet* was going to be pulled? In fact there was little advance warning of the release of "I Am The Mob". As a result, a possible chart-topper was sadly jettisoned to pop's also-rans.

"I Am the Mob" also had two good songs on the B-side. "'My Selfish Gene'," explains Owen, "is all about how man is really selfish (referring to the book *The Selfish Gene* by Richard Dawkins). It's either uproariously funny, or very, very sad. It depends on which way you look at it."

It also ended up on the *International Velvet* album (eventually six songs were released off the album in single format). Two songs had therefore been released four months in advance of the album. Previously, a similar fate had befallen singles released from *Way Beyond Blue*. For this to happen once to a band is unusual, even in this industry, for it to happen twice is virtually unheard of. It adds support to the arguments of those who thought that Catatonia could easily have been on their way out.

"Jump Or Be Sane" is a popular piece in the Catatonia repertoire, and has stood the test of time – a successful mixture of dark verses and a bouncy chorus. There is a line in it, *Be not vexed by remorse, I'm not lost, but one who has gone before,* which is actually taken off a gravestone in the churchyard next to Monnow Valley studio in Monmouth.

The video for "I Am the Mob" was filmed in Scotland under the direction of *Twin Town* director Kevin Allen. It was his first attempt at pop videos, and the idea was to be slightly different to the usual pop video format.

They thought they'd include a bit of piss-taking in it to show that they were not entirely serious about "putting horses heads in peoples' beds." That was the idea behind Mark having a little boat to play with and Owen going fishing. There was also a guy playing bagpipes in the video.

"That was Cerys," explained Owen. "This guy turned up with his bagpipes, and I think he thought he was going to play bagpipes for us, but it was the actual bagpipes we wanted. He taught her how to hold them and she marched up and down with them."

The humour extended to putting Aled's drum kit in the water with goldfish swimming in it. This was an homage to Keith Moon (The Who) who also put goldfish in his drum kit. Both drummers used identical drum kits.

One poignant shot in the video shows the group playing cards in a cottage. The camera zooms in to a card in Cerys' hand to show they were playing Happy Families. It was barely twelve months since the split up of Mark and Cerys.

The working atmosphere on the video was very laid back and took just two days to shoot. The group were in control of the project. They knew what they wanted and they achieved it.

A 13-gig tour to promote "I am the Mob", (the original intention was also to promote the *International Velvet* album) occupied the band from October 9th until November 4th. In addition, a pre-tour secret gig was played at Betws Y Coed, on October 7th. The gig at the Swallow Falls pub was not really advertised properly by the band in the hope that they could have one quiet gig. It was in the local papers and a board was nailed to a nearby tree simply announcing "Band Tonight." It was also posted on the internet on one of the unofficial websites devoted to Catatonia.

The pub is situated halfway up a mountain by a waterfall, very much in the home territory of Mark and Paul. It was also the venue of a secret gig the year before.

Owen predicted that the upcoming tour was going to be a very good one. For her part Cerys insisted, "I am trying to be a bit more cultured this year, especially on tour." Manchester has hosted some memorable Catatonia gigs and October 17th at the Hop and Grape was no exception. After singing "Bleed", Cerys threw herself off the stage into the middle of the crowd.

The security guards did not seem to see the funny side and one of them, along with the tour manager, pulled her back from the audience. Back on stage, as though nothing had happened, she kissed the security guard – drank some lager and carried on. It was her first experience of stage diving and still looking bemused Cerys added, "I just thought 'fuck it'. My skirt wasn't there when I actually got back on stage. I still had my fishnets on. They were ripped to shreds, but at least I still had them on." So much for being cultured.

The encore was outstanding, with Cerys performing an acoustic version of "Tourist" (disproving all she says about not being able to play the guitar) with an added ending especially for any *Songs on Sunday* devotees. "There's a hole in my bucket, fuck it."

Owen had good reason to remember another venue on the tour. The Reading Alley Cat has a pillar in the middle of the stage which he had walked straight into at a previous gig. So, this time he was on his guard. It was also on this tour that Owen began his singing career with the band. While rehearsing "International Velvet" the band reached the chorus, *Everyday when I wake up, I thank the Lord I'm Welsh*. At this point, Owen was told that he should be singing as well.

At least the album was being showcased and the new songs were well-received. The release of *International Velvet* was originally set for October 27th 1997, but it finally saw the light of day on February 2nd 1998. Only a three month delay this time. Someone must have had growing confidence in the band.

The title *International Velvet* was chosen because they wanted something romantic that was also broad-reaching to match their ambition of making music that a lot of people could get into. It is also the title of one of the songs on the album that had Welsh lyrics. However, the effect that *International Velvet* was going to have on Catatonia could not have been predicted.

Mark felt that the album "just sounds more like an album". Even though it was written and recorded in six to eight weeks it was more cohesive and confident than *Way Beyond Blue*.

One of the songs, "Goldfish and Paracetamol", a collaboration between Cerys and Paul, was the first song that she had written in six months. Often suffering from writer's block she is appreciative of the songwriting input from others in the band. It was the start of the decline in the number of Matthews-penned songs on Catatonia records.

Recording the tracks at Monnow Valley gave a warm ambience, even though part of the album was mixed in London where the mood was more stressed.

According to Owen, "Everything was laidback and countrified and it's got a completely different feel to it. And also, because we're all used to living in a city, if somebody takes you out of that and puts you in the country, you feel like a different person straight away."

The incident Cerys remembers most about recording the album is, "probably the day I went swimming in the river, naked, on a pink inflatable hippo. I was floating downstream, and I turned the corner and there were all these scouts on the river – 'Hello boys.'"

Summing up the differences between *Way Beyond Blue* and *International Velvet,* Cerys was of the opinion that there was a new maturity and confidence in terms of every aspect of the band. From the way that her voice had changed over the years of touring, to how the five members of the band worked together.

International Velvet was helped by the fact it was produced by Tommy D who had worked with Catatonia on "You've Got A Lot To Answer For". He'd followed the band's live gigs, so he knew what they wanted to achieve, probably more so than Stephen Street who had produced *Way Beyond Blue*. After recording the album, it became quite clear that this was a step up. Cerys was confident they had progressed and that the new album was more life-based. Recording over a definite period had been an advantage. She added that "Strange Glue" was her favourite.

From here on, it was becoming more apparent that Cerys was comfortable singing material written by Owen. The dynamics of the band had been in a state of flux and Owen's songwriting qualities were emerging.

Welsh Bands Weekly reviews releases by signed and unsigned Welsh bands as well as conducting interviews with band members. Cerys was interviewed prior to their London Astoria gig on November 4th where she said about *International Velvet,* "The sounds in it vary more. We've got quite rocky ones like 'I Am The Mob', we've got other ones which are more vocal, and some folkier ones, so it's more of a mixture just to confuse people. There's one, which is just vocals round a mad drum roll. There's 'Why I Can't Stand One Night Stands', and 'Johnny Come Lately'."

While the members of the band were not dispirited, progress was still slow. Very little interest was being shown in them and things had gone quiet. So much so, that many people thought they had split up. Even though the band thought it was a great album, there were doubts as to whether people would understand what they were trying to do. Indeed, the review in the November 8th edition of *New Musical Express*, seemed to show just that. "Catatonia were never going to shock you musically, but rarely has a canter for the middle ground been so unseemly."

For their final live performance of the year, Catatonia headlined a benefits gig at Cardiff Students Union on 29th November. Organised by Cynyrchiadau Ann Fon and Ffilmiciu Eyriol as part of a special evening to mark International Aids Day on Welsh channel S4C, other artists were Davy Spillane and Frances Black. The tickets were good value at £5. However, something special was in the melting pot.

Shortly before Christmas, the band recorded the video for the song that was to change their lives. The video featured Rhys Ifans, who played one of the Lewis twins in *Twin Town,* and his girlfriend. Directed by Kevin Allen (brother of Keith), it was shot in TJ's nightclub in Newport (a popular venue for Catatonia), St Arvans service station in Gwent and on the Severn Bridge. The days of borrowing the toll money to cross that stretch of water were about to be blown away.

It was business as usual at TJ's as the 60ft Dolls, old friends of Catatonia, were waiting to soundcheck while Catatonia filmed the stage sequence of the video, which featured a stage dive where Cerys retained her clothing.

TJ's regular Marc Casnewydd of Newport was an extra at the filming and as well as being amazed that the band actually played and sang live throughout the recording, he remembers several of the boys in the crowd shouting for Cerys to stage dive. On consulting the director, he surprised Cerys by telling her to go for it. He was supposed to say "No."

So, with all the crowd egging her on and joking about it, she agreed to stage dive. She was counted down to the dive a couple of times, but at the last minute she screamed and hid her eyes. The boys at the front were encouraging her and the other members of Catatonia added "Go on Cerys, you can do it." She responded with a massive dive into the audience.

The live segment of the video took around four hours to film, with breaks in between. During takes Paul sighed, "It's funny, every time we release something we always think, 'Yeah! Fucking hell, everybody will love this. Maybe they'll go for it this time'."

The atmosphere was upbeat and friendly and Marc recalls being pleasantly surprised. "I asked her [Cerys] to pose for a photo for me and she did. But more than that, she made an effort. She put her arm around her friend, looked straight in the camera and smiled – a great big superstar smile. She's a great girl. Really nice and down to earth. Almost like a friend, like a sister. I really did like her."

During the recording of the album, Owen had not been certain about releasing "Mulder and Scully" because, "I think we've got things there that are more representative and more deserving of being singles." Within a few months he was pleased to be proved wrong.

The song's title seemed to intrigue people who thought it was in some way directly connected to the *X-Files*, and Mark admitted that, "It's just a blatant attempt to finally get us in the charts, so we don't get dumped."

As soon as Cerys could get away after Christmas without upsetting her family, she took a bus to Chamonix, and spent the New Year holiday period at a friend's house in the South of France. Even though she admits she's crap at skiing, she got some practice in on the slopes. Unaware of it at the time, this break would allow her to re-charge her batteries for the onslaught that was to follow.

1997 had seen Catatonia continue their quest to gain chart success and pop fame. However, on paper they were still major league under-achievers at a time when the British music scene was in a state of lethargy. Trying to explain the reasons behind the failure to breakthrough Cerys said, " I don't know really. I really don't know. I know what I think – how strong our songs are – but then it doesn't come out like that. Before *International Velvet* we might have been dropped."

It was that close.

But then. Is that someone knocking at the door? Is that really Dame Fortune?

EVERYDAY WHEN I WAKE UP,
I THANK THE LORD I'M WELSH

We don't listen to anyone else at all as regards our music. Doing that is the first mistake you can make when it comes to making records. We have always been confident about what we do.

Cerys Matthews

One of Cerys Matthews favourite songs is "Somewhere Over the Rainbow" by Judy Garland. 1998 was to provide Catatonia with their own rainbow. After floating aimlessly in the calm waters of nineties British pop music, they were now to take it by storm.

"I was sure it would happen in 1993, and then I thought 1995 would be the one," admitted Cerys. "I don't like even numbers see, so when it didn't happen in 1997. I mean, eight for God's sake. Eight is my least favourite number."

Catatonia started the year with a tour, this time to promote *International Velvet*. A total of 18 gigs were scheduled, starting at the De Valence Pavillion in Tenby on January 7th and finishing at the Electric Ballroom in London on February 5th. They continued the practice of taking upcoming Welsh bands as support acts – on this occasion Dererro. In fact, the original intention of the band was to concentrate this tour on Wales, with a desire to play places where other bands never played. However, it was finally decided to go ahead and tour outside of the Principality as well.

On a personal note, I was now confident that I had won my battle with myself. What I had heard from Catatonia during 1997, particularly towards the winter, had convinced me that this was it. I had been "an orphan in the storm" that they had unknowingly rescued. I knew they had been the catalyst in kick-starting my recovery. Gone now, were the fears of losing my lifeline.

I could now view the band in the same light as a proud parent does its child's achievements. There are some times in your life, when you know that – 'this is it'. I had been all over the place to see them, I had made great friendships on the way. It had not all been plain sailing, and there had been setbacks, but gradually I had pulled through. I had regained my self-confidence and esteem and much, much more. In short – I was back.

For this tour, as usual, I was determined to take in as many of the gigs as I could, and there was an optimistic expectancy that had been brewing up for the past few months. First port of call in 1998 was to be Tenby.

I like to read if I am travelling on public transport, although over the past few years I had largely given this a miss. I had picked up my copies of *Melody Maker* and *New Musical Express* for the journey. Ashley Bird, in *Melody Maker*, made the following observation about Catatonia.

"Now with a new single and album ready for release, they are poised to make 1998 their own. These gigs (*International Velvet* tour) will be the start of a year that will see them surge into indie music's premier league. They will take up residence in the Top 20, and everyone will wonder why they hadn't noticed them before, you can bet on it. This will be the year that sees Catatonia become real pop stars. Don't miss."

This was crystal ball journalism of the highest order.

In the following issue, surprisingly, Steve Lamacq admitted he thought Catatonia were becoming a little tame, too safe sounding to deliver the "big thrill."

Quite a few music journos had expressed surprise at "Mulder and Scully" and *International Velvet*, considering them interesting but never really contenders.

Some ventured that the rest of the band had now finally caught up with Cerys' undoubted vocal ability. Certainly, there had been many gigs when the band had led from the back. Cerys has always had a good voice, but the band had developed the fine art of contending with her missing and mixing words, lines or verses out of songs.

The beauty of Tenby contrasted starkly to the dire weather. It was not a day to take photos for the summer holiday brochures. In retrospect, it seems odd in the year when Catatonia were to make their impact on the British pop industry, that they should start in this 400-capacity venue, in Cerys' beloved Pembrokeshire, with a below par performance.

She appeared to be high and the band wore sombre black. Their attire, the weather and the "atmosphere" in the theatre almost convinced me that I had accidentally strayed onto the set of a Hammer horror movie.

During the gig, "International Velvet" failed to rouse the almost comatose audience. It was almost as if that there was an undertaker's convention in town.

Mark concedes, "Oddly enough it is one of those songs that goes down really well in England, because they see the sense of humour. We played it in Manchester and they loved it. Maybe there's more Welsh people in Manchester than Tenby."

For whatever reason, Cerys' voice seemed to falter. Complete with encore, they only played for 65 minutes. One member of the audience got a smiling, good-natured, "Fuck off you," from Cerys, while most of the others were in various stages of rigor mortis. Vultures circled above. Had I travelled over 300 miles for this?

Afterwards, Mark was charitable about Cerys' performance. "She's paranoid she'll lose her voice on the first night. Last tour, we had to cancel a couple of shows."

Cerys admits to having become, "a bit stoned really", and was clearly unhappy about the show. "It's because I sang yesterday on the video shoot and all the time on playback, instead of miming. I can't help it."

I stayed overnight in Saundersfoot, before trekking back to Sheffield via Swansea the next day. I knew I'd seen them play better, but I was getting very familiar with the contents of *International Velvet* and was convinced this was the beacon to a bright future.

That night, irrespective of the lifeless response of the audience, my stance finally changed. My confidence was fully back. Put it down to my post-Catatonia gig adrenaline rush, or maybe a dodgy meat pie in Tenby, but I could not sleep. I chose to walk around Saundersfoot – a place I do not know well. It was very dark and it was pissing down with rain. I found a small chapel and I sat down in the entrance. Unashamedly, I found myself crying for quite some time.

I did not thank the Lord for my becoming Welsh – changing that is beyond any divine power. But I did thank the Lord for being alive. Through the band who I had called 'fucking bastards' the first time I heard them, I had discovered Wales, a country whose people had played such a part in my recovery and whose countryside really did offer a welcome to me. As a bonus, I was captivated by the sheer wealth of music that I had found there, in every city, town and village I visited. Then a sodden, mongrel dog brushed up close to me as I leant back against the chapel door, it gave me a loving smile and then dropped the smelliest fart ever delivered by a canine. At least it ensured a prompt return to my hotel room.

The next gig was Saturday the 10th in my hometown at the Sheffield Leadmill. Since my love affair with Wales began, never had I wanted to return home so much. This was it. For one person there, this gig was *the* big one. The band I had been telling everyone was one of the finest live acts I had ever seen, was playing in my own backyard. It was to be the first night of the rest of my life.

No more was I to take refuge at the back or out of the way. It had taken time to get here from being mentally and physically broken. I had travelled around Britain and crossed the continent watching this band. In four and a half years, I had met many people from all walks of life who had become friends and I had visited scores of places that I would never have seen. I had been like a hermit crab, slowly coming out of my shell, taking in the sights and sounds and then creeping back in the shell. Now it was possible for me to say, "bugger the shell". It had been, to paraphrase a popular song, a case of "The winner takes it all, the loser gets fuck all" – I was finally sick of being the loser.

The Leadmill and Catatonia are as good a recipe as you will get for a gig and a good night out, and I found out later that Mark loves the place too.

The atmosphere of pending success was intoxicating, unlike the previous gig. The minute the boys appeared and Cerys floated onto the stage it was as though I had been kissed by an angel. Then I remembered how it was this particular angel that had caused me to disappear rapidly in Wolverhampton when she had appeared close to me. It only seemed like yesterday, yet in a sense it was a lifetime away.

The songs and tunes sounded so much more beautiful that night. For the first time in my life I was on a non-induced trip. I had paid good money in the past to float this high.

There was the odd heckler who was dispatched by a smiling Cerys, as she sexily purred, "What's wrong baby? This one's for you."

She went through all the emotions that night. From her tongue-in-the-ear rendering of "Strange Glue," to a house brick in the face "I Am The Mob".

After the gig I walked the streets of the city centre and surrounds. I looked at places in the eerie moonlit backstreets and neon-bedazzled thoroughfares. Many memories danced on the stage that was my mind. Most of them were tangos of pleasure, but there was the odd waltz of chagrin. Sheffield had been a good partner to me, the soul mate of my youth. It had been a long, sometimes turbulent relationship, but the flame had been only weakly flickering of late. My new mistress – Wales – was beckoning. I had to go. It would take time. There were things to do, but I would leave.

On January 12th Catatonia played at Joseph's Well in Leeds. Once again, Cerys herself was the subject of some personal attention. A sneering punter spent the gig pulling faces and sticking two fingers up at her. She just fronted him and seductively cooed, "Oh come on honey. What are you doing that for? Hmmm. What you flicking the V for, honey?"

The guy instantly folded. Cardiff 1, Leeds 0.

I was beginning to wonder if this guy was the same one from the previous two concerts. Was he a plant? Or perhaps he was a genius? Had he thought of a way to get the sexiest singer in British pop to give him a personal audience every gig?

Cerys has developed her own way of coping with onstage confrontation.

"The more hassle and feedback I get, the better I react to it. The best gigs are when you've had some interaction. If you don't get any you feel a bit disappointed with everyone there and they probably feel a bit disappointed with me."

She'll be enjoying this tour then, I thought.

They left audiences at the other gigs on the tour in no doubt that they meant business. With their ability to combine old favourites along with songs from *International Velvet*, they were irresistible. With guitars and drums weaving the intricate slow ballads, and then accelerating with total precision into the stomping anthems, Cerys dominated the stage with a mixture of awesome venom and gossamer tenderness. This was a band making a statement, "You can't stop us now!"

Mark was still not that confident. "I don't think we fit in with what's going on. It's not something you can pin down as easily as you can with certain bands of the last few years. We're quirkier. There's something lurking under the surface."

"Every band is different," concluded Cerys. "Some are good and some are bad. But I do this because I'm on a fantasy thing. Because of the clothes and mostly because I love singing. But we're going to have a brilliant time. Fucking hell, we're not stopping now, we've kept going this long."

Possibly, these were the final decrees of the reigning King and Queen of the underachievers.

It was eventually decided that "Mulder and Scully" would be released on January 19th. The B-sides on the CD were; "No Stone Unturned", "Mantra For The Lost" and "Mulder and Scully (The Ex-Files Remix). A 7" vinyl and cassette were released with "Mulder and Scully," and "No Stone Unturned." It was to chart at number 3. It was also *Melody Maker*'s Single of the Week.

Melody Maker commented further, "It pisses a glorious shower of contempt on Catatonia's contemporaries (Sleeper/Echobelly/any other young guitar band) or indeed any other single this week, from a great height."

The record was originally given B-list status on Radio 1 but was quickly promoted to the coveted A-list, and was the "Screamer of the Week" on X-FM's breakfast show. More media coverage on the Welsh S4C TV *I Dot* show followed. As did their national TV debut on Channel 4's *TFI Friday*. TV appearances on BBC TV's *The O-Zone, Live and Kicking* were accompanied by Radio 1's *Evening Session* and the *Simon Mayo Show*.

There was an appearance and interview on *Fully Booked*, which gave viewers a taste of the Cerys Mathews media technique. On being asked "if she ever thought she would get as famous as she is?" She replied, "Yes, always."

Some people later complained on the BBC pop teletext *Vibe* that she was being arrogant. First, it was a truthful answer, but not for the first time in her career, she was upsetting people by not giving the reply they expected. Second, there is a distinct difference between arrogance and self-belief.

Cerys was not enthusiastic about the obligatory appearance on *Top of the Pops*. "I didn't enjoy it much actually. I didn't feel very at home."

Some critics labelled "Mulder and Scully" a novelty record, while others kept linking it to the *X-Files*. These comments irritated the band, but there was a silver lining because for the first time they were regularly to be heard on daytime radio.

Mark believed that the title of the song was a key factor in its success. Having considered "Stop What You Keep Doing" and "I Can't Sleep Alone", criticism of the final choice did not worry him. In the end, they just thought, "Fuck it, let's just call it 'Mulder and Scully'."

Words from Aled are as likely as an appearance by Cerys at a meeting of the Order of Rechabites. A contender for the thinnest book in the National Library of Wales at Aberystwyth would be "The collected speeches of

Marcel Marceau, Chico Marx and Aled Richards." It is for this reason I enclose this quote.

In a group discussion about "Mulder and Scully", Aled commented, "In a relationship, do you find yourself not washing or brushing your teeth as often as when you started out. You know what I mean? And then it's like they won't come near you."

The rest of the band stared at him and said nothing. Drummers are very surreal.

When Cerys heard that the song had come in at number 3 she was, "…in a taxi with this amazing guy, who's done a lot with charity for Cuba, and he was talking away about what he'd done, and I'm going, 'Shut up. Put the radio on. That's me. I'm on the radio.' I'm never very cool like y'know. It had got to number 3 and I got out the taxi and laid on its bonnet. All over the Cuban flag and everything, y'know."

After the trials and tribulations of the previous few years, she was entitled to feel elated. Cerys admitted that her delight made her act, "like a tart. I still get very excited about things like that." (She later claimed that she'd spent a couple of grand with her friends, restaurant and club hopping until her credit card was stopped).

But she was not the only one to toast success. Owen confessed to almost drinking his entire bodyweight in champagne.

Back in Sheffield, there was one very proud man. The fact that my belief in the band had been justified hardly seemed to matter. I quickly got used to comments like, "How did an old git like you, spot a band like this?"

All those miles of solitary travel; the time spent in cold and damp bus and railway stations; the panic attacks; rain sodden festival grounds; they suddenly seemed like the best days of my life. And yet it was as a result of trying to take my life, that I had come across these "fucking bastards". My senses were numb with pleasure.

Catatonia were the flavour of the month, and it seemed everybody wanted to have them on their programme. They appeared on Radio 1's *The Late Show* and played sessions on GLR, Virgin radio and ITV's *This Morning*.

The latter programme appealed to Cerys' domestic psyche. "It was great, only I didn't get to meet Judy. I love that kind of thing. I want to go back on it and do some cooking." Unsurprisingly, no-one was brave enough to let Cerys read the Weather News!

In January, Cerys was a front cover girl for *Melody Maker*. This was a pointer for the year ahead when she would appear on nearly as many front covers as the bar code. She would grace amongst others; *Melody Maker* (twice more), *New Musical Express*, the *Mirror's* Friday Supplement, *The Guardian's* Weekend Supplement, *Hot Tickets* (London Evening Standard), *FHM, Select*, and *Q*.

The album *International Velvet* was released on February 2nd on CD, cassette and vinyl formats. The first 5,000 CDs were in velvet bags and have become very collectable, whilst the LP was a 1,000 limited edition 12" vinyl (it now commands prices of upwards of £50). It debuted at number 11 in the album charts.

International Velvet features the tracks; "Mulder and Scully", "Game on", "I Am The Mob", "Road Rage", "Johnny Come Lately", "Goldfish and Paracetamol", "International Velvet", "Why I Can't Stand One Night Stands", "Part Of The Furniture", "Don't Need The Sunshine", "Strange Glue" and "My Selfish Gene".

It was received warmly by the critics; "It must be simply genius," *The Times*. "Buy It!" *FHM*. "Catatonia's music is simply sublime," *Time Out*. "Bloody Essential," *Melody Maker*. "Soulful, soaring genius," *NME*. "One of the finest guitar singalongs for years," *Vox*.

Yet the band thought they were done for with *International Velvet*. Two weeks before it was released, people were panicking, saying 'it's not going to do anything.' There was hardly any publicity at all.

Reporters were curious about the title of the album and Mark was asked if the title song could be a new Welsh National Anthem?

"Probably not," he replied. "The melody's too difficult to have them singing it in the streets at closing time." He concluded that not everyone in Wales would like it, because essentially the song contained a lot of cliches about what it is to be Welsh, and took the piss out of Welsh culture. People who were inflexible about the Welsh language would not like the Welsh poetic meter it was written in, and English people might not like the chorus.

Following the band I had became increasingly fascinated with their Welsh lyrics and "International Velvet," gave me the boost to start learning Welsh. I have studied French, Greek, and Russian in my time, so I thought Welsh would be no more difficult. Wrong!

Working on *International Velvet* had also allowed Catatonia the opportunity to demonstrate their technical skills. Paul programmed the track "Why I Can't Stand One Night Stands" at his home studio and when they went to the recording studio it sounded so good, they kept all the original programming. "Goldfish And Paracetamol" was made there too.

"Johnny Come Lately" was produced in a small, 16-track studio in Cardiff called Big Noise. Then they tried it again in the bigger Rockfield Studios, but it never had the feel of first one. The decision was made to keep the original version and add little bits to it.

Having toured the UK, there was still a need to promote the album to a wider audience, and continental Europe was next on the itinerary. The London Calling Festival was held at the Paradiso Amsterdam over February 13th and 14th with Catatonia once again being one of the featured acts.

They were supporting the Stereophonics on the 13th. The set was going well, but after completing the fifth song "No Stone Unturned" Cerys left the stage, seemingly in tears, shortly followed by the band. We were later told that she had lost her voice.

Catatonia's recent success made them popular guests at the Brit Awards in February 1998. A symbol of pure hedonism, Cerys danced the night away, mainly on the top of the table. She professed to totally enjoying the evening and was really excited at being in the same room as artists like Tom Jones, Robbie Williams, All Saints and the Spice Girls. She went into overdrive dancing along to a duet sung by Robbie Williams and Tom Jones.

Cerys had appeared on the Space album *Tin Planet* singing "The Ballad of Tom Jones". Space thought so highly of the collaboration that on February 23rd, the song was released as a single.

As a result of the long time spent touring together in 1996, the two bands had become good friends. They shared a good sense of humour and respected what they were both trying to achieve musically. I was amazed, therefore, to read in another biography that Tommy Scott (Space) was terrified to ask Cerys to record it with him. Tom Jones was a hero of Tommy's and he had always wanted to dedicate a song to Jones, so he wrote the song with Cerys in mind because he was certain she could sing it in the style of Nancy Sinatra.

Cerys had no inclination that it was going to be released as a single, but when the idea was mentioned to her she "went up to Liverpool to see them play, had a big night out and did the song the next day with a really croaky voice."

Tommy Scott was asked in 1999 if he felt he deserved any credit for Cerys Matthews success after the duet. "I don't think so," he replied, "we were nothing to do with it. That song would never have existed if Cerys had said no… We never used them and they never used us."

The video too was one of the better ones of 1998, featuring a car hanging over a cliff, with Tommy clinging to the bumper, and Cerys taunting him from the bonnet of the car.

Cerys and Tommy Scott appeared as guests on the BBC pop quiz *Never Mind The Buzzcocks* on February 23rd to coincide with the release of their record which was to chart at number 4.

They were also interviewed on the *Pepsi Chart Show* after performing the song, a feature of which was a live satellite hook-up with Tom Jones in the USA. During the cross channel chat, Tom Jones revealed that in the earlier days of his career, he sang under the name of Tommy Scott. It was obvious that Cerys was thrilled to speak with her hero, and for once she looked shy and bashful.

"I've got a million questions to ask you," Cerys said to Tom Jones, "I've just done a duet with a guy called Tom. Could I do one with you please?"

Afterwards she said, "It was one of the highlights of my life," and she celebrated with a £1,000 bender.

Happily for Cerys, the duet was to materialise at the end of the year. Who was the singer who said, 'If you don't ask, you don't get?' I wonder...

Publicity was becoming food and drink to the band. A story appeared in the *Sunday Mirror* at this time relating how Cerys had turned her back on drinking after a paragliding incident nearly killed her.

"I lost control of my glider one morning after a heavy night out. I got in a bit of a tangle with the ropes. I didn't think I was in any real danger at the time, but afterwards people told me how close I'd come."

Cerys has admitted several times that she is not enamoured with flying and the fact that the story did not feature anywhere else was reason enough to doubt about its accuracy. The thought of Cerys waking up in her terraced house after a night on the booze, looking out of her window and thinking, "What a nice day. I'll get my wings from the cupboard under the stairs and fly over Cardiff Bay for a while," did amuse me. Of course, the story was untrue.

As for her giving up drinking, well, I have just seen a pig fly past my window without the assistance of a glider.

Time spent at home was to be in short supply now, particularly for Cerys who was undertaking a high volume of promotional chores.

At this time she was house sharing with sculptress Angharad Jones – who once built a 45ft vagina out of scrap metal.

It was a happy refuge for her as well as being the venue for wild partying. Their garden was populated by non-vegetable type occupants, assorted

Above: Early days at The Legendary TJ's Club, Newport, South Wales.
Photo: David Hardacre.

Above: A poster for the gig at Clwb Ifor Bach, May 1, 1996, the last time Catatonia played at their local club.
Below: Opening night of the *International Velvet* tour at Tenby De Valence Pavilion, Jan 7, 1998. (l-r) Mark, Cerys, Paul.
Photos: David Hardacre.

Above: Cerys at the Phoenix Festival. *Photo: David Hardacre.*

Left: Owen on stage at Tenby De Valence Pavilion, Jan 7, 1998.
Above: Cerys in typical pose, Reading Festival, August 24, 1996.
Photos: David Hardacre.

Left: The tour to promote "I Am The Mob" and *International Velvet*,
Aberystwyth University, October 18, 1997.

Above: Catatonia discuss tactics seconds before taking the stage at the Aberystwyth
University gig, October 18, 1997. (l-r) Cerys, Mark, Owen, Paul, Aled.

Below: Author Brian Wright, Cardiff Bay, April 2001.
Photos: David Hardacre.

Above: Supporting the Manic Street Preachers at Cardiff International Arena, December 21, 1998. *Photo: David Hardacre.*

sculptures by Angharad, mingling with Cerys' increasing barmy army of garden gnomes.

"I know it's not very rock 'n' roll, but I've got about six hundred," laughed Cerys. "They're starting to take over the house."

Using her ingenuity she invented a game called Millennium Gnome to try and control their numbers. Apparently, the idea was to put some of the gnomes on the garage roof and try and knock them off with champagne corks.

The band was now spending a lot of time in London, but typically it was not all work. Some of the band and crew attended a karaoke night at The King's Arms, a popular gay pub in Soho. Cerys went down a storm singing "I Got You Babe" with her radio plugger, earning the makeshift duo tremendous applause from the pub's customers.

Now that the band had gained a wider audience, their exploits were being recycled by a grateful press, although sometimes a different approach was made by the interviewer, such as the time that Cerys was asked if she would give up sex and alcohol to keep on singing.

"Strange question," was the reply. "I probably would, though. But you can drink and sing and have sex at the same time. So my answer is Byddau wastad eisiau caru ond gorau I gyd yw caru rhuw ac alcohol ar yr un pryd, – (I will always want to sing, but, best of all, is singing, sex and alcohol at the same time.)

Cerys' pop star quality was attracting media attention on a lavish scale. She was a natural for the limelight and lapped up the attention. Her personality had captivated the most ardent of reporters and they wanted to dissect and examine it, to find out what made her tick. The rest of the band was equally content to keep out of the glare of publicity. They were happy for her to be the main focus, but were also concerned that handling the media alone might get her down.

One journalist observed, "She exudes a flirtatious streak that always shines through in public. You have to fancy the naughty street-wise side of her personality. She would almost certainly out-drink you in the pub and still be well in control to drag you home and give you the best seeing to you are likely ever to have."

Life accelerated at helter-skelter pace for the band. Video shooting for "Road Rage" took place on March 13th (Friday) under the direction of Gerald McMorrow. The theme was the band playing in a room at the top of a skyscraper overlooking a futuristic Cardiff. There were monkeys in the room and small spaceships/cars outside. Cerys sported a stunning £800 Copperwheat Blundell designer trouser suit for the shoot.

Making expensive pop videos is not one of her favourite pastimes, although this one gained her approval. The fact that, "they cost ten times as much as it does to make an album, just for a three-minute bit of footage" is a strong bone of contention with her.

The end of March saw the band play the Radio 1 1998 *Evening Session Tour*. Catatonia, Travis and Idlewild played five gigs at Glasgow Barrowlands, Manchester Academy, Leeds, Birmingham and finished at the Newport Centre on March 26th.

With *International Velvet* selling well and beginning to catch on, it provided them with another vehicle to promote the album. The bands and the Radio 1 crew gelled and the overall atmosphere on the tour was very good.

Cerys became friends with Fran Healy (Travis) and his mother, and after the Manchester gig Brian McClair (then of Manchester United) joined in the guitar entertainment in the dressing room. He left before he could become another player from the club to feature in a Catatonia song.

Appropriately the tour finished in Newport, the scene of a good few Catatonia gigs. At a previous show, Cerys had acquired some underwear. "I had Welsh flag boxer shorts thrown at me. They had, 'from the boys from Maesteg' written on them." Newport is also the town that first brought the Welsh music scene to the general public's attention after Neil Strauss from the *New York Times* labelled it "the new Seattle".

Prior to going on stage, Cerys spent time in her dressing room showing off her latest acquisition; a small classical Spanish guitar which she'd bought off Fran Healy for £20. (He'd bought it for only £10 a few days previously). It gave her the chance to sing the soft, Spanish folk songs that she had learned in her youth, while simultaneously warming up her voice.

This was almost a hometown gig, and they were greeted on stage like heroes returning from the Crusades. "Is this the new Seattle then?" Cerys enquired to be greeted with chants of "Wales! Wales! Wales!"

A few songs into the set, a floating condom is passed over the crowd into Cerys' waiting hands. "That's not very romantic? I'm a lady. I thought it was a balloon," she said in mock disgust, which betrayed a ball-chewing grin.

After the gig, Owen flitted between friends and Radio 1 suits analysing his performance. He commented, "At one point someone at the front shouted, 'Owen, you wanker!' but then I suddenly realised I was, so the lad had a point."

Nine days later, a ten-date European tour gave the band the opportunity to further enhance their reputation on the continent. The tour started at Brussels Botanique on April 4th and concluded at the Knaak Club in Berlin on April 15th.

Cerys remembers spending part of her 29th birthday on a Belgian garage forecourt, despite the fact that Belgium is not one of her favourite countries. "The toilets are filthy. There's pornography everywhere you go. Dirty men at railway stations."

I had whetted my appetite at the Amsterdam gig, so I thought I'd hop over the North Sea to take in some of their European concerts. I used the Hull to Zeebrugge ferry to avoid getting my feet wet, and as we sailed past Spurn Point, I looked at the sparse grassy strip of land surrounded by water and immediately thought of Glastonbury on a good day.

I took in the gigs at Brussels Botanique and Copenhagen Vega. The gigs were enjoyable and it was a trip down memory lane hearing "This Boy Can't Swim" again. Continental gigs were ideal for me as I was now enjoying talking music with anyone as well as checking out the trends and styles in vogue in other countries.

Then, as Catatonia headed to Scandinavia, I made my way leisurely to Hamburg where the band were to be playing in eight days time. I took the scenic route from Copenhagen and arrived at Hamburg via Cologne.

I found myself exploring the railways, picturesque steel works, marshalling yards, coal fields and slag heaps of Germany. I met some friendly locals who always seemed to be telling me I had come the wrong way, and would shake their heads in disbelief as I set off again, almost certainly in the opposite direction to where I'd been instructed.

Eventually, I reached Hamburg. I must have tasted every brand of lager and schnapps available on my travels, as well as a huge variety of sausages, which frankly did not appeal to me. But, in the end, the show was worth it.

By now I had decided to use the Hamburg to Harwich ferry home instead of following the band to Berlin for the last gig. Knowing my luck, I would have ended up in Prague.

I returned home to find that those bastions of British journalism, the *Daily Telegraph* (April 16th) and the *Sunday Times* (April 19th) had printed features on the band. Fame and favour were coming from all directions.

Stardom had well and truly arrived for Catatonia and the media courted its new sweetheart with passion.

"I feel more tired sometimes," Cerys admitted. "It's a cliché that the front person gets more attention, but it's true. And I think we're all aware of that in the band. But if I was watching us, I'd be more interested in watching all of us and seeing how we work together. Then, maybe I'm just a boring muso."

Difficult as it is to take your eyes off Cerys, it is still fascinating to watch the band as a whole. Mark will occasionally do a moonboot stomp, always in a straight line, either forwards or backwards; Owen will vary between windmill arm actions and helicopter spins; Paul will chew along in time with the music, while Aled auditions for the Llanelli Buster Keaton (the great stone face) impersonator championships.

Celebrity invades the private life of those it affects. Cerys was now getting recognised when she was out shopping which made her become very self-conscious. So much so, that she dyed her hair black. Previously, her thoughts had only extended to trying to sell a few records and getting them played on the radio. Public recognition was something that had been dreamt about, but the reality of it took a while for her to adjust. Could Maxi-Homebrew Matthews handle the transformation to Champagne Cerys?

"A crucial part of life is squeezing every opportunity out of it," she enthused. "We've worked really hard for years to get here, who wouldn't enjoy all the trappings once they arrive?" Prior to 1998, Cerys' main claim to fame was having the same hairdresser as Bonnie Tyler.

In a feature for *Sky* magazine, the photographer wanted to take a close-up of the boys, but was having difficulty getting them to smile. Cerys was asked to say something to make them laugh, and she let rip with a stream of impenetrable Welsh. It worked. When asked what she'd said, she laughed. "I told them to get their cocks out."

Another story goes that a certain magazine belittled Ffion Hague, using her Welshness as the source of ridicule. The next issue was to feature an interview with Cerys, during which she answered all the questions in Welsh.

Around this time Cerys was asked to record a song for a short film, entitled *Anthrakitis*, which was set in a Welsh mining village, directed by Sara Sugarman for Tiger Lily Films. Cerys sang Ivor Novello's "Keep The Home Fires Burning" for the project.

It was an interesting venture for her because the song was from the First World War, and Cerys had heard "one of the old boys do it in my favourite pub in Pembrokeshire. Then I would go home and sing it with my auntie, who was 86. That's how it should be. Anyway, we recorded it with banjo, drums, harmonium, and tuba. Fantastic."

A song of a completely different nature, "Road Rage", was released on April 20th. It had been delayed by a fortnight to allow more radio and MTV airplay prior to its release.

It appeared in CD, 7" vinyl, and cassette form. B-sides for the CD were; "I'm Cured", "Blow The Millennium" and "Road Rage (Ghia mix). The record made Radio 1's A-list. Its highest chart position was number 5. It was also once again *Melody Maker* Single of the Week.

It was this song, probably above all others recorded by the band, that will prove to stand the test of time and be regarded as one of the classic UK hits of the nineties.

"Despite not replicating the success of 'Mulder and Scully' this follow up won out because of its greater subtlety and finesse," enthused one critic. "Cerys cooed and a million hearts liquefied."

To promote the single there was more radio and TV work. Cerys and Owen went on *The Big Breakfast*, Cerys did a radio phone-in on Mark Goodyear's programme while the band appeared on the TV show *Fully Booked*. All this publicity gave *International Velvet* a futrher boost in the album charts.

On the *Jo Whiley Show* Cerys appeared with Ian Brown and Ian McCulloch. She recalls admiring Ian Brown's gold medallion and the both of them playing her toy guitar, but she admitted to not knowing what the hell Ian McCulloch was talking about. The show was enjoyable for Cerys because it puts the participants on the spot, whereas she found the heavily scripted *Never Mind The Buzzcocks* programme boring, because there was time to practice the answers.

The Catatonia ethos of "Have tour, will travel" saw them headline a series of eleven gigs in the UK under the banner of Ride The Tiger. It started at Llandudno, North Wales Theatre on April 18[th,] and should have finished at the L2 in Liverpool on May 4th, but that gig had to be cancelled as Cerys was unwell. So the final gig was at Shepherds Bush Empire, London on May 1st.

Fans who went to the gigs on the Ride The Tiger tour were not disappointed. There was no way that success was going to allow complacency to affect their performance. Llandudno's North Wales Theatre staked its claim for a place in the history of Catatonia. According to Cerys, "When we played Llandudno, it was the first place the audience had ever sung along with the Welsh words to 'International Velvet'."

The gig was a sell-out. Mark, being from North Wales, had been a little wary of this night. His parents, relatives and old schoolmates came to watch and there was a fear that if he forgot to talk to any of them, they might have thought, 'Who the fuck does he think he is now?'

They interrupted the tour to appear on *Later with Jools Holland* on April 24th. Cerys commented that, "It was a complete treat to be able to just sing with no drums and no guitars, (referring to "My Selfish Gene", where she was accompanied by Jools Holland on piano and Paul on bass).

The UK video for "Mulder and Scully" was not deemed to have been suitable appeal for US audiences, so on May 2nd Catatonia went to Windsor to record a video featuring Cerys running through a city of filing cabinets attempting to find the rest of the band. The party after the Shepherds Bush Empire gig went on so late and the video shoot started so early the next morning that Paul decided against any sleep that night.

By now, the Catatonia bandwagon was really on a roll and they signed up to Vapor Records, a subsidiary of Warners in the US. The company was run by Neil Young and his long-time manager Elliot Roberts. Young had been a former headliner on the prestigious HORDE tour of the USA and one of his first actions was to place Catatonia on the 1998 tour beginning in July and August.

A press pack describing Catatonia and their songs was issued to spread the word about the band. Cerys described themselves as being "like other Welsh bands. We have a reputation for enjoying life and like most bands really, we're the last people to leave the pub or stop talking about music."

In the press pack, Cerys once again referred to the fictional meeting with Mark saying, "I met Mark when I was busking, because I had a guitar string missing and he gave me one."

No doubt, the double entendre of the quote was not lost on her.

The album *International Velvet* was released in America on May 19th on CD and LP, with the same track-listing as in the UK. The forthcoming HORDE tour was seen as an excellent opportunity to promote the album, but there were other European commitments closer to hand.

For two rescheduled continental gigs at Barcelona Bikini on May 6th and Madrid Ktdral the next day, "Acapulco Gold" made a rare but welcome return to the set list. Following the last Spanish gig, after being dropped off at the airport Cerys hadn't a clue what to do. With everything having been organised for her over the past few months she suddenly felt help-less. From being a totally independent person, she had become hopelessly dependent.

Clearly, it was time to take a vacation, and the chosen destination was Ibiza. Just the ticket for a shy, retiring Cardiff girl. She checked in at San Antonio and began to look for her brother who was also on holiday there. When she found him they went to an Irish pub with a karaoke bar. The place was full of British people and Cerys got "very, very drunk."

She was talked into singing and somebody put "Mulder and Scully" on the karaoke machine. The customers eventually realised who she was and started taking photographs. The stage was on wheels and halfway through the song it gave way, causing her to "end up on the floor right on me bum, legs in the air, flashing my knickers and laughing my head off." It was to provide the inspiration for the song 'Karaoke Queen'.

While Cerys was on holiday *International Velvet* reached number 1 in the album charts on May 10th. It was only to stay there for one week, but it was selling consistently well. Understandably Cerys was delighted, but initially she did not believe it. It took her the best part of a day on the tele-phone to confirm the information. When that mission was accomplished she carried on drinking and enjoying the rest of her holiday.

On returning home, "I got a letter from the bank saying, 'Miss Mat-thews, due to the unnatural abuse of your card, we're writing to you to warn you someone may have stolen your card.' "It's quite nice to know that your bank would notice this increase in spending. Nice one." And then she promptly binned the letter.

The media hype surrounding Cerys was intensifying but she was revel-ling in the attention that had once seemed so far away. Naturally, romance and her love life were questions people always asked about, but she never gave away any information that would jeopardise any ongoing relation-ship.

Melody Maker asked her if she would rather be single and thin, like in "Mulder and Scully". Her reply was that she was single and loved being single... "I've got a lovely house, gorgeous friends, a job I absolutely love and adore. Why would I want anything else? I'd just rather slip in and out of the pleasure pool."

It was soon to be out of the pleasure pool and across the pond.

Many British bands have died in the USA and despite some reservations, now was the time to put in some promotional groundwork for Catatonia's Stateside exposure on the summer HORDE tour. At the end of May,

Cerys and Owen went over to the US to give interviews to magazines such as *Spin, Rolling Stone* and *Raygun*. Ever a glutton for punishment, Michael Krugman of *Raygun* magazine took another opportunity to talk to them.

Cerys was in the kitchen preparing a cocktail and welcomed him.

"Nice to meet you," she says.

"Actually," he replies, "we met last year in Texas. You called me a cunt."

"I must have meant it as a compliment."

"And that's how I took it."

The interview traced the origins of the band before Krugman informed them that there would be a lot of hippies attending their forthcoming summer HORDE tour.

Krugman also reminded them that the band had given interviews where they had slagged off the USA. Cerys defended their stance explaining, "It's the whole McDonalds mentality that puts me off." She stressed that they didn't know the good things about America yet. She expressed hope that Catatonia would fit in somewhere. With increasing experience of the media, it was evident that odd moments of diplomacy were appearing.

Having concluded the publicity work it was then back to the UK for more gigs. They played a festival on June 6th at Cheltenham racecourse, which was arranged by the local Student's Union. Catatonia and 60ft Dolls were supporting Space. No doubt when the gig was arranged, the band order was correct, but events in 1998 made a mockery of such things. Not that Catatonia begrudged Space their headline. As for the weather that day – basically it pissed it down. Needless to say I was there.

Over the past two years, Catatonia had earned a reputation as being one of the best festival bands. "Stealing the limelight" – was the message coming through loud and clear. Two outdoor gigs in London's Finsbury Park, also featured Catatonia. First there was an invitation to play *Madstock*, (obviously headlined by Madness), that had come about as Catatonia had also supported them four years previously. Second *Pulp in the Park* which saw my home-town band at the helm. Catatonia were superb at both concerts. If they'd entered the Grand National in 1998, they would have strolled it. Perhaps, even Sheffield Wednesday could have won matches with Catatonia in the side.

At such one-off festivals and gigs, there is less pressure. It is easier to belt out the songs because Cerys' voice is not suffering the results of singing for several consecutive gigs. An additional bonus for her at these two festivals was that a lot of her friends had come down and they all had a really good time together.

Europe once again welcomed Catatonia that summer. Lisbon was the setting for Expo '98. At a festival to celebrate this event on June 17th, Catatonia provided a support slot. The gig went well and they were given such a warm reception that it prompted Cerys to rate this festival as her favourite European gig. She had an affinity with Portugal "a mad place – complete disregard for rules."

Paul had brought his daughter Gwen to the festival and everyone celebrated her first birthday at the Expo. Cerys got the crowd to sing "Happy Birthday" and the incident was recorded in the national press the next day. While they were there they also filmed part of the video for "Strange Glue." Continuing the publicity drive, Paul took time out to give an insight into his craft in *Bassist* magazine.

The hectic pace continued and Catatonia added more prestigious European gigs to their roll of honour. On Saturday June 20th, they played the Rockpalast festival at picturesque Loreley, Germany in the company of Garbage, the Beastie Boys, Pulp, Asian Dub Foundation, Sonic Youth, Money Mark and Rancid. Their eight song set included "Dead From The Waist Down", which according to Cerys in one interview was written a month or two later! It was a performance in keeping with the surroundings and Cerys was resplendent with her favourite fashion accessory – a gemstone worn on her forehead in the Asian style. It was also a personal triumph for me as I actually managed not to get lost.

The success achieved by the band during the first six months of 1998 was nothing short of phenomenal. Life as a celebrity fitted Cerys Matthews like a glove. Her delight was clearly obvious when she was in the company of someone famous whom she admired, such as Tom Jones. She was like a kid on Christmas morning.

Tens of thousands of people were now very much aware of the band who just a few years previously had been trundling along in a transit van to play gigs in front of thirty fans on a good night.

MY STAR'S ASCENT A CERTAINTY

*I never questioned it no matter what anyone told me. I was just born that way,
I guess. I'm very determined.*

Cerys Matthews

Prior to 1998, Catatonia had a loyal fan base in the UK and a good reputation in continental Europe. The success of the preceding six months provided them with a whole new audience, particularly in the UK. However,
pop music is a very unpredictable and uncertain industry. It can be a very
risky business trying to capture worldwide markets without consolidating
the reason for success – the home market.

The question remained as to whether the band could handle the fame
and add to their achievements or buckle under the strain. In the UK things
could not have been going better. The band were riding on the back of
two top ten singles (three in Cerys' case) and a number one album. Festival
crowds were now being wooed, even though some of the band remained
unimpressed by open-air events. Leading up to the Glastonbury festival in
1998, Cerys stated, "I'm sure Mark will remain as staunchly anti-festival
as ever. Festivals and all that kind of liberalism shakes him to the ground."
After missing out on playing the previous two years at this venue due to
bad weather, their luck changed.

Catatonia took to the "other stage" at Glastonbury on Friday at 10pm.
Cerys, wearing a skin tight sparkling gold dress and a viagra-dispensing
grin, took control from the start. She even took time out while singing

to wave to familiar faces in the crowd. At previous festivals some criticism had been directed at the band for playing obscure B-sides but this time it was mostly favourites only, plus the newly-penned, "Dead From The Waist Down".

The crowd was soaked, so Cerys enquired, "I hope you're not too cold," and later told them to "pretend you're all on a hill, under the stars, in Sri Lanka. You're all drinking margaritas."

Luckily, the rain had stopped just before Catatonia came on stage, Cerys coping with a bin bag on her satin heels. The band was amazed at the sheer volume of people singing along with the tracks from the album. Owen remembers, "We were all caked in mud, the tarpaulin's flapping away and our sound man says to us, 'I haven't a fucking clue if anything's working so just get out there and enjoy it!' We did."

Cerys strutted the rain-soaked stage with her customary shuffle 'n' shimmy dance routine. She even went walkabout during "Sweet Catatonia". Her stage dancing was now becoming a feature of the act, but can be a touchy subject. Some less kind critics have likened her dancing to that of a farmer, a barmaid, Tina Turner or a knock-kneed lad in stilettos. On a more positive note, it is this joyful enthusiasm that captivates the crowds.

One individual who was captivated was Festival organiser, Michael Eavis, who came to watch the group with his daughter and declared them the best band of the whole weekend.

Immediately after their performance, the band had to fly off to another festival, this time in Denmark. At a press conference prior to the festival, there were people from Latvia, Lithuania and Poland, praising the band for charting in their countries. Owen had been unaware that they had even released records there adding, "The fact that you can communicate with people in those countries without ever having been there is quite a thing to get your head round."

Despite the frequent comments that were being made about the wardrobe of Cerys Matthews, Catatonia were invited to play a four-song soundtrack as star guests at Donatella Versace's fashion show in Milan. An elegant range of pret-a-porter bin liners for exclusive festival use were conspicuous by their absence.

The band was all dressed in black Versace, except Cerys. They considered singing "I Am the Mob," although wisely decided against it, being in *The Godfather's* home country. Owen was not enthusiastic about the gig. "I'd rather be remembered for writing great songs than for how much we can steal off fashion slags."

It was though, a measure of their progress.

"The lifestyle we've got is one of extremes anyway," accepted Owen. "One minute you're being chauffeur driven to a private opening of a Versace shop with two bodyguards, the next minute you're stood outside Cardiff station with your bags in your hand going home. I mean, six months ago, we wouldn't have been allowed in that shop."

The next single off *International Velvet* was "Strange Glue", released on July 20th on CD, 7" vinyl and cassette. The B-sides on the CD were "Road Rage" (Live from Shepherds Bush) and "That's All Folks".

The song initially went on Radio 1's B-list, but was quickly upgraded to the A-list. Its highest chart position was number 11. An added bonus was that *International Velvet* climbed back up the album charts to number 3.

The accompanying video, shot in black and white by George McMorrow, turned out to be one of their best. Rarely has Cerys looked more beautiful. The video portrays her as the old films used to capture the stars, somehow projecting an image whilst still evoking a feeling of mystery about their persona. Unusual in as much as Cerys is seated whilst singing, she has to use her hands to coax every ounce of emotion from the song. This is cut with shots of the band taking in the sights of Lisbon, and playing on stage and interacting with the audience. The final touch shows Cerys and the boys leaving the stage. If I was consigned to a desert island and only allowed one video, it would be "Strange Glue".

The song itself has a history. In 1996, Owen had told of seeing "something in Aberystwyth that said – 'When faced with my demons, I clothed them and fed them. And smile when they're taking me over'." These words must have inspired him to write this song as they are featured in the lyrics.

Another story attached to the lyrics concerns Cerys singing the song. She often does not change the "she" to a "he" because she likes to really feel the words. This led to some fans speculating about Cerys' sexual preference. Cerys has never ducked the issue of enjoying sex – with men. I find it difficult to comprehend the logic of people who think she is "on the other bus" just because of a song's lyrics.

To promote "Strange Glue" Cerys and Owen turned up on the rather austere Radio 4 programme *Woman's Hour* on July 22nd for an interview and an acoustic set, which was followed later by the group appearing on BBC TV's *Lottery Show*.

The increase in TV work in particular had a downside for Cerys; "We've been doing a lot of telly work lately and when you mime it's fooling the public. I hate it."

Not surprisingly, the album *International Velvet* was nominated for the Mercury Music Prize in the last week of July. At least there would be a chance for Cerys to sport some of her newly acquired Versace wear at these forthcoming awards ceremonies.

The year also saw a milestone in my life in the shape of my 50th birthday, thereby shattering the belief that "the older you get, the wiser you become." Because I had a good collection of Catatonia memorabilia, the choice of a suitable present with some relevance was causing a few people some problems. I did not have any bodily adornments or tattoos. So it was decided I was to have a Catatonia-themed tattoo. I wanted it to feature the whole band but apparently that would have overstretched the budget so I had to settle for one of Cerys.

The tattooist had a minor problem. He had never heard of, nor seen Catatonia. But, working from a photograph, he produced a brilliant portrait. A tattoo is something I had never thought about having before, but if it had not been for the band then there would have been no arm to put it on. Word must have got around the fans and I was really surprised at the number of people who want to see it, even kiss it, at gigs.

Cerys' taste in clothing and other adornments was continuing to provide interviewers with a topic of conversation. In July, *New Musical Express* remarked that the current look was love beads and ethnic baubles and asked if she was basically a hippy.

"Fucking hippies," she protested. "No I'm not, because the word 'hippie' these days conjures up dope-headed, lazy cunts… I just like to think the better of people, rather than the worst and work from there. I believe in discipline, knowledge, and structure. You have to have rules so you can rebel against them and forge your own personality and culture. So, I'm a hippie with a cane."

The hippie look could just have been the costume for the forthcoming trip Stateside. The quirkiness of managing bands was demonstrated when the group was shunted off to the USA after the release of the single "Strange Glue." Many other acts at this point in their career might have stayed at home to promote their new record to the hilt, but not Catatonia. Most of their UK audience had been aware of the band for six months or less. They were in huge demand at home, but at a crucial time it was decided to send them Stateside. The opportunity to really capture the home market and establish them as a supergroup was not taken. Nevertheless, Catatonia connected with the HORDE tour in late July, but not before Cerys had expressed on Radio 1 that she didn't want to go and had told her management likewise. The band was reportedly more keen to get into the recording studio to lay down their next album.

Despite these reservations Catatonia left for the USA, almost certainly following pressure from their US record label. The objective presumably was to promote *International Velvet* and to try and gain a foothold in the US marketplace. Why then use the HORDE tour? In all probability the reasoning was based on the success of several British bands over the years joining the Lollapalooza tour and gaining from the huge exposure. However, this tour comprised a varied mixture of bands, many not familiar to British fans. Owen's initial reaction to being told, "You're playing with Blues Traveller" was, "That must be great. To be honest with you, none of us know anything about Blues Traveller. What do they sound like?" Their spots on the tour were to be equivalent to ten minute jamming sessions, hardly suited to Catatonia's style, nor was it ever going to be long enough to help promote the album, which supposedly was the reason for them going. It wasn't in any way like the festivals that they had become accustomed to.

Surely, someone must have been aware that this was more likely to be a means of preventing Catatonia enhancing their reputation rather than assisting them. Somewhere along the line a grave error of judgement had been made in trying to promote Catatonia and their style of performing on a tour such as this. They gigged in places such as Mansfield, Holmdel, Scranton, Wantagh and Bristow. This was like trying to bring an up-and-coming American band to British music fans' attention by getting them gigs in Gillingham, Scunthorpe, Withernsea and Barrow-In-Furness.

However the band made good use of the tremendous amount of time spent travelling on the tour due to the long distances between the venues. To relieve the tedium, Owen organised delivery of a little Akai 12-track digital recorder, which enabled them to lay down some material in the back of the tour bus. It was preferential to "just sitting around watching films or whatever."

They managed to hook a microphone up and over from the bus ceiling, which kept swinging about while they were in motion, so it was necessary to move around to catch up with it while singing. This determination to keep writing allowed them to demo some new material on the tour bus and gave them excellent preparation for going into the studio to rehearse and record the album *Equally Cursed and Blessed* in September.

Mark did not like the tour at all. "Tragically we found ourselves argy-bargying about stupid things, like who's carrying the equipment." The circuit took in Canada as well as the USA. "We did this gig in Toronto," (July 28th) said Cerys, "where there was hardly any stage, no barrier, no nothing. I was face to face with the audience, thinking, 'Fucking hell!' It's been years since we'd done that… well 13 months. It was quite scary until we got into it and the sweat started dropping from the walls. But I know Mark loved it. It's more like the Clash and less like Steps."

An under-age fan, Heidi Kronhert from Picketing in Canada, along with some friends, were grateful to Cerys that night, for sneaking them into the licensed gig.

"I like people with a bit of… presumption, is that the word?" said Cerys, "You know, don't ask, don't get, and they asked."

Cerys' comments about the Canadian gig were telling. Thirteen months previously, a venue such as that was stock-in-trade to the band. Over the past year Catatonia had conquered virtually every major European festival and charted in most of those countries. They had numerous prestigious TV, radio appearances, promotional events and awards ceremonies behind them – and suddenly they land in the US where they are unknown, low down the bill, in out-of-the-way towns, playing shortened sets not suited to their style in tiny, sweaty venues. Obviously it took a bit of time for them to come to terms with their situation. Having finally struck pay dirt in the UK the last thing they wanted was to be a support act on a bill of this kind.

When Catatonia had finished their part in the tour, they were scheduled to headline two concerts; one in San Francisco, the other in Los Angeles. Paul was unable to play these gigs, which resulted in the San Francisco gig being cancelled and a session musician filling in at the Los Angeles Troubador on August 19th.

They then returned to the UK for the back end of the festival season, when Catatonia played the twin venue V98 festival, appearing at Chelmsford on Saturday 22nd and Leeds on Sunday 23rd August. A tabloid reporter previewing V98 wrote, "Cerys is great, but I hope they get an early slot as I wouldn't let her loose near alcohol for too long."

Also, her fashion sense for the festival was called into question by a *Melody Maker* writer who thought the Tommy Hilfiger trousers she wore were revolting. "They make people smile," she replied disarmingly, "they make me laugh myself."

Cerys did not wear the same outfit at the Mercury Music Prize presentation evening held on September 16th. The theory behind this kind of award is no doubt sound, but many of its critics consider it a backslapping exercise for the trade. To try and select the best record from the top twenty selling albums of any year, would, in itself, be a frightening task.

But sales is not the criteria applied. For every album that has achieved success, there is another one chosen that beggars description. Suffice to say, Gomez won with an album allegedly made in a garage. When it was nominated, my understanding was that it had sold just over 21,000 copies, whereas *International Velvet* was a double platinum album.

Catatonia were to be rewarded for other endeavours, however. *Welsh Communicator of the Year* is an award given to the person or persons, who in the eyes of the members of the Institute of Public Relations in Wales have done the most to promote Wales and Welsh interests. In 1998, it was awarded to Catatonia, the first time it had ever been awarded to anyone other than an individual.

The crystal bowl was presented to the group in Monmouth where they were recording the new album. "This is actually the first award we have ever been given," said Cerys. "We've been nominated in quite a few music awards, but this is the first we actually won, and it's great that it is something so closely related to Wales – diolch yn fawr." (thanks very much)

Paul considered the award was, "for generally raising the profile of the Welsh language".

The album *Equally Cursed and Blessed* was co-produced by Catatonia and Tommy D at Monnow Valley with the final touches applied at Whitfield Studios in London.

The band had been keen to record new material and set out to produce songs in a different format to those on the previous album. The idea was to present songs that they considered more petulant, fresh and yet at the same time moody. The inference was that while *International Velvet* was mainly about relationships, *Equally Cursed and Blessed* would be about a broad range of subjects such as insights into the human condition, the aristocracy and high street prams.

The entire band contributed to the writing and Cerys warned that some fans may be in for a surprise with its diverse range. She laughingly referred to the lyrical input by stating, "I've got a history with Mark, and I love that boy to bits, but he must be twisted… He writes about tampons and DIY gynaecology."

In the opinion of producer Tommy D, "They're exceptional songwriters, all the band members. They're quite finely tuned in the art of songwriting. The albums [*International Velvet* and *Equally Cursed and Blessed*] were recorded at Monnow Valley for two reasons," he continued. "Firstly, it is quite local for the band, secondly, the vibe there is amazing too. It's a tremendously calming place. It was Paul, having started jamming along to 'Bulimic Beats', who suggested to get Elinor Bennett to play harp on it, and the great thing about doing vocals with Cerys is she's always 'on it'. We did vocals at two in the afternoon and then we did vocals at four in the morning. 'Shoot The Messenger' was done at four in the morning when we were fucked-up because we knew that the sound of the vocal had to be rasping and out of it."

The content of *Equally Cursed and Blessed* was in a state of flux during the making. Provisionally a Welsh song "Dwr Yn Yr Afon" and the experimental "Gibber Artist" were going to be included, but these did not make the final version.

Aled discussed another gem that did not see the light of day. "We've got a Lewinsky and Clinton song. But, if we don't bring it out in the next month, we'll be buggered." (I wonder if this was a version of the Sheffield Wednesday anthem – Going down, going down, going down?)

While making the album, Cerys encountered spirits of a non-alcoholic persuasion. "Monnow Valley Studios is an old mill house outside of Monmouth. The boys knew this room was haunted, but nobody told me. Everything was fine for eight weeks, and then I heard someone calling my name and they touched my leg. I couldn't see them. I truly believe in ghosts, so that's probably why it happened. I moved rooms after that."

There was not a lot to do in Monmouth in the breaks during the recording, but a return to her home city was on the agenda as Cerys went to see Tom Jones in concert at Cardiff International Arena and after the show met her hero close up and managed to acquire a souvenir of the occasion from his dressing room. There was a bright pink pair of knickers that had been thrown on stage by Tracey from Barry, which Tom had used to wipe his brow with, but these were now the property of Cerys, who stated that she was not going to wash them.

Also at the gig was Kelly from the Stereophonics, whose record "The Bartender and the Thief" had just charted. This prompted Cerys to buy some celebratory champagne for the after show party, which resulted in both of them getting pissed, but not before they had tried doing handstands and other inebriated gymnastics.

During recording, it transpired that the album was not the only thing that had been cut. "The woman who owns Monnow Valley recently discovered that I'd carved 'Catatonia' on the mixing deck," confessed Cerys. This transgression did not stop the studio grounds being selected as a photographic backdrop, because Cerys had been chosen to be photographed in a set of moody poses for a forthcoming photo exhibition celebrating 100 years of Welsh culture.

The theme of photography and culture was further developed when *Melody Maker* once again had Cerys as its cover girl on the October 24th issue, prior to the release of their next single.

She was wearing a necklet featuring a penis and testicles. She explained this in her own familiar manner. "I like cocks, that's all… We've all got these bits and we all like using them. I like having a cock around my neck."

When she was told it was nice to see the male organ getting a good press, she responded; "What! Cocks don't get a bad press! Testicles get a bad press, but oh! No, I love them. Sorry, I'm quite sexual and I like sex."

It might be considered a cock-up to release five singles (and six songs) off a twelve-track, best-selling album, but those on high determined that "Game On" would be released on October 26th. It came out in CD, tape and 7" vinyl formats. The B-sides on the CD were "Mulder And Scully" live from Newport, and "Strange Glue" live and acoustic from Radio Four's *Woman's Hour*. "Strange Glue" was the only B-side on tape and vinyl. It made the Radio 1 A-list, and became the first song of the band to be put on the X-FM A-list. Despite this, it reached a highest chart position of only 33.

This release not only tested the loyalty of some fans, it also failed to boost sales of *International Velvet*. Obviously, those who bought "Game On" were either new fans who had not bought *International Velvet* or confirmed Cataholics.

On the decision to release this record, Cerys explained, "Half the band didn't want five singles off it. Half didn't give a shit. I didn't give a shit. All I want is to be able to keep singing and write good songs. I've got pride in that." I know it is not compulsory for fans to buy records, but this rather flippant attitude appears to be out of character for Cerys, who normally enjoys an excellent rapport with the band's fans.

There was minimal publicity surrounding the release of the record and no video made, which suggested the record company did not consider it a project worthy of investment. It only highlighted what seemed to be an idle and unimaginative business venture aimed solely at relieving the fans of their money. If the idea was to keep Catatonia in the public eye, then they had far stronger material in their repertoire. The right song could have pushed the group back firmly centre stage and consequently a greater opportunity to maximise the potential sales of singles from the next album could have been grasped. It would also have raised their profile at the ensuing awards ceremonies and increased their chances of winning most of them.

The band promoted "Game On" on *TFI Friday*, *Top of the Pops* and *Ant and Dec*. Cerys was also scheduled to be a guest on Clive Anderson's TV chat show, but this was cancelled for production reasons by the BBC.

Catatonia were then invited to sing at the *Prince's Trust 50th Anniversary Concert* to be held at London's Lyceum Theatre on October 28th. The original plan was to sing "International Velvet" with a 100-strong Welsh male voice choir providing the backing. At the last minute the band pulled out amid confusion as to what had prompted this move.

At the time, a spokeswoman for Catatonia and the Prince's Trust blamed a lack of rehearsal time due to the band working on the album. The tabloids latched on to anti-monarchy remarks that Cerys had made in a radio interview and claimed that the band was snubbing Prince Charles.

Cerys later explained the real reason. They believed in the Prince's Trust and considered it a good charity and that was the reason they had agreed to do the gig. The organisers seemed more intent on emphasising Prince Charles 50th birthday and wanted to edit "International Velvet" and include a circus of Welsh tap-dancers and singers. The band had wanted it to be a treat but felt they could not perform under those conditions.

This was followed by a statement issued by a spokesman for the Prince's Trust which stated, "It was just one of those things. We were sorry they didn't perform on the night, but we're really happy that they're supportive of the Prince's Trust and what we do. We look forward to working with them in the future if their schedule allows."

The Prince's Trust was virtually the only event they missed as the end of year awards ceremonies were looming up. In the *Q Awards*, Catatonia were nominated for Best New Band and Best Single ("Road Rage"). They won the award for Best Single. At the ceremony itself, when Cerys collected the gong on behalf of Catatonia, she stunned the audience by dedicating it to 'disgraced' ex-Cabinet Minister, Ron Davies.

"This is nice. Thank you very much. It's a bit too early to say anything really, isn't it? Why couldn't we have been last? I've only had two glasses of champagne. This one's for Ron Davies. What the hell were you doing?"

Q magazine acknowledged that "the song boasted the most frequently chanted chorus of 1998, and had been a factor in Catatonia's transformation from minor league indie band to festival conquering heroes. Samey and sturdy in equal measure, it surges from husky, sexual predacity into strutting 'sod-you-tossface' defiance. A boisterous pop nugget with typically lung-shredding r-r-rasping vocals from Cerys Matthews – musically, sexually motivated first lay-dee of Welsh pop."

Allegedly, "Road Rage" was nearly bumped from the album by the band in favour of a rude song about Warners USA. Thankfully they reconsidered.

Cerys was interviewed by Jayne Middlemass on BBC TV after the presentations. "I had such a long speech planned," shrugged Cerys over a drink, "but I wasn't going to thank anyone. If you want to be thanked for being in this business, then you're in the wrong business. You're a lucky bugger. Tonight I met Bob Geldof. He's much more gorgeous in the flesh than I ever imagined." Jayne then informed Cerys that Bob Geldof was just around the corner and had heard every word she had said.

The next issue of *Q* magazine featured Cerys on the front cover along with Michael Stipe and James Dean Bradfield. She was also to be featured on the cover of the Christmas edition of *Melody Maker*. It seemed you couldn't look in any rack of magazines in the newsagents without seeing Cerys looking back at you.

It had been a year of fantastic achievement for the group. They were now reaping the rewards of their labour. Acclaim and success though, seemed to mean different things to the individual band members. Mark remained sceptical. The thought of fame and demands being made on him did not appeal. Owen just could not believe it at all. "It's like watching a film of another band."

Cerys was ecstatic and could barely conceal her happiness. In 1998, all her dreams had come true. She had met her heroes, sung with the best acts in the world, and at last there was good money coming in. What was most special for her was that her family was thrilled for their youngest daughter.

Away from music, in the autumn Cerys became an aunt when her sister gave birth to a son, Ewan, and she rated one of the highlights of the year as being her Granddad winning the "Neath in Bloom" horticultural contest.

She did treat herself towards the end of the year when she bought her first car. An MGF. "If it hadn't been for my MG, I'd have gone crazy. When I put that fucking key in the ignition, I'm away. Fantastic."

But the year's activities were far from over. On December 14th, Crai re-released the two EPs "For Tinkerbell" and "Hooked" on a single CD entitled *Catatonia 1993/1994*.

New Musical Express and *Melody Maker* were both cynical about this release, and considered it to be a way of cashing in on the band's success, although the *NME* acknowledged that it proved that "there was something precious there all along." *Melody Maker* though considered that, "you'll chortle warmly at the dreamily anaemic "New Mercurial Heights" and "Dimbran.""

I didn't.

It is always a dangerous exercise to compare a prototype with the finished product. The two songs mentioned are special to a lot of Catatonia fans. To this day the band are capable of mixing 'in your face' songs with 'sat on your lap' ballads. But, if it were not for Rhys Mwyn and Crai, the world could easily have lost out on Catatonia.

A pedantic point. On the original "Hooked" record, the song title is spelt 'Difrycheulyd," whereas on *Catatonia 1993/1994* it is spelt "Difrychewlyd."

The recorded album, *Equally Cursed and Blessed* was about to be mixed when Catatonia were scheduled to tour again. Such had been their success that in December they were "very special guests" supporting the Manic Street Preachers on a twelve-gig arena tour, starting at Bournemouth International Centre on December 8th and finishing at Cardiff International Arena on December 22nd. It would be the first real opportunity to showcase some material from the new album.

They looked forward to the tour with their fellow countrymen. "We don't go round each other's houses or anything," said Paul, "but, I dare say we'll get to share some time on this tour."

The tour started quietly at Bournemouth on December 8th. The next day should have been a day off, but it was to be a busy one for Catatonia. *Jools Holland's Hootenanny* New Year's Eve broadcast was recorded at the BBC. The show featured the band, as well as a duet with Cerys and Tom Jones singing "Baby It's Cold Outside".

Cerys met Tom Jones' family and really enjoyed the duet, saying that it was one of the highlights of her year. She thought the song was a classic and rated the earlier version by Ray Charles and Betty Carter as brilliant.

December 10th saw Catatonia arrive in Sheffield. Cerys sat in her dressing room sipping water, preparing for the gig, and likening the venue to "the bloody Ideal Home Exhibition." Possibly due to pressure of work, Cerys had not checked the itinerary in advance and claimed she didn't know it was going to be an arena tour. However, there were compensations,

"We love supporting people, 'cos the pressure's not on you at all and you're in the bar that much quicker."

She fronted the band wearing a silver sequined top and dark combats and launched into "Storm the Palace", a song described by *Select* magazine as "a pounding call to arms, that takes in punk energy, a Motown backbeat and a vocal like Belinda Carlisle after a night on the gin."

That night Catatonia were beset with technical problems. The official line was that they did not get a sound-check, but as I waited outside the auditorium, someone with a voice remarkably like Cerys ran through something like "Storm The Palace" and a few other songs complete with backing.

Cerys attempted "Goldfish and Paracetamol" as an acoustic solo. First time round, after playing herself in, she sang nothing, as she had forgotten a song that she had co-written. She ventured a second attempt and was about to falter again when she cried, "Help me, help me, God."

God sent his messenger Paul to retrieve the situation. He leapt up and frantically gestured towards Mark. As if on cue, the backing kicked in and Cerys sang the song word perfect. Amazingly, a lot of people had not noticed there was a problem in the first place.

At one point, Cerys admitted, "We haven't a clue what's next." We, the audience, hadn't either, but such was Cerys' spell, that I doubt if anyone cared.

The final song was "Strange Glue". As Owen played the haunting guitar introduction, he glanced to his right expecting to see Cerys taking up the vocals. She was, however, just finishing a conversation backstage with Aled. Owen continued the intro. Cerys turned and walked to the front and came in bang on cue, second time around. Pure theatre. A manufactured band would have died on the spot.

On the night, they got a tremendous reception from the crowd. When people say Cerys should go solo, they should consider that she is not the easiest singer to accompany, nor would any other band of musicians get the best out of her vocal talent.

Not that the band are incapable of making the odd mistake. Paul recalls that Mark plays guitar and keyboards on "Dead From The Waist Down", but at this gig he ballsed it up completely. He played the keyboard out of tune and hit so many wrong keys, that eventually he stood back and held up his hands in surrender. It was all captured on the big video screen.

"And he immediately sacked himself the next day," added Owen.

The number of Catatonia gigs and festival appearances I have seen runs into three figures. I pledge that the first time they play a perfect gig then I will never go to see them again. In fact, if they get near a perfect set I will do a Cerys and invade the stage.

In *Select* Magazine Cerys gave a reason why she sometimes forgot the words to a song, "…strange things – like being in Sheffield and they're singing in Welsh – I find it difficult to remember that I'm meant to be singing…"

Diolch, Cerys.

The band interrupted the tour on December 13th and flew down from Glasgow to London to appear at the *Smash Hits Poll Winners' Party*. The only 'alternative' outfit there, they mimed "Road Rage" for a screaming crowd of over 10,000 teenage girls and their mums.

Cerys thought, "It'll be good preparation for Christmas at home."

Paul was concerned that as it was a mimed show, it was a bit of a shame, since for those kids, it would be the first concert that they would see and might think all gigs are the same.

It was then straight back to pick up with the Manics again.

Throughout the tour Cerys' voice gave her problems, and there were concerns that the Wembley appearances might be affected.

"The only pain in the neck for me is my voice," she has admitted. "Because of the constant touring, I have developed cysts on my neck, which means they can get inflamed. I do tend to strain when I'm singing. That's the only pain. Everything else I love."

It was incredible how her voice stood up to the workload it endured in 1998. It faltered throughout the tour, but not to the extent of spoiling the performance. With all the interviews, on top of the concerts, and defiantly refusing to mime, she somehow kept going.

Clearly, Cardiff was the place where Catatonia wanted to finish the year. Cerys asked the audience to join in "International Velvet" and "Road Rage" and her voice was getting croakier. But as the audience responded, Cerys came back to them, ripping the sinew out of her vocal cords. I watched the rest of the band closely at the final gigs and they musically and vocally offered Cerys an easy way out. She did not take it even though the support vocals were stronger than usual.

A very tight group is one that knows each other's strengths and weaknesses. Many of the acts that have charted between 1997 and 2000 probably have no idea what I'm talking about. But why should they? I am talking about bands like Catatonia who have served their apprenticeship on the road.

Here was a group that has never bothered about which square on the stage to stand in. I've seen them when just standing on the stage seemed a difficult enough feat. They haven't had to learn poncey dance routines. They have not sought refuge in music because they got pissed off playing in soap operas. They can handle most situations or problems on stage.

Catatonia manufactured themselves. Only genuine musicians can.

I saw them at Sheffield, Newcastle, Glasgow, Exeter, and twice at Cardiff CIA on the tour. Every time I was down at the front. During this tour I had my hair cut. I made a bet that I would next have it cut when Wales won the Rugby World Cup. (Because they failed in 1999 I have been told that I will not be held strictly to the bet. If a band that I work with gets a record deal, or Catatonia has a number one single, then I can have it cut.)

* * *

A few days before the Cardiff concerts I went to a gig at a working men's club in Tumble, Carmarthenshire. There were two school bands, Asteroid and Doli, supporting Big Leaves and Topper – the crowd a mere 40. When Big Leaves took the stage at Margam Park only five months later, I looked around me at the 30,000+ crowd and thought of that night. You never know what is around the corner.

I awoke each day now, grateful to be here. 1998 had been a good year for me. My passion for life had been back with me for a little over eighteen months. My very existence, which once I had put no value on, was now so precious. I still enjoy a drink or six but it does not control my life in the way that I had forced it to.

It had been a remarkable twelve months for Catatonia. An overnight success that had taken nearly five-and-a-half years to happen. The seemingly endless gigging and touring, the development of their songwriting and musical talents, and the vocal prowess and stage presence of their singer had all come to fruition.

Did the group deserve to be where they were?

"Oh yeah," said Cerys. "Absolutely. And the thing is, '98 was the best year of my life. I could die happy tomorrow."

Getting there is, however, only part of the battle. The problem is staying there. For a band that had endurance engraved on them, you would not expect them to slip away quietly, but the year's schedule must also have been physically demanding both as individuals and as a group.

There had been ominous signs too. The poorly-timed attempt to break into the USA and the lamentable decision to release "Game On", which effectively slammed the brakes on their steamroller success at home, were both portents of a plummet in UK record sales.

Clearly, a year like 1998 would be difficult to repeat. If 1999 did not offer the same highs then the critics would be hovering like vultures. Progress can take many forms and it takes time. Patience was now the watchword for Catatonia.

I CAUGHT A GLIMPSE, AND IT'S NOT ME

There was a time when we had to get the train from Cardiff to London, and I
couldn't see the train. It was then I knew I had to stop.

                                                              Cerys Matthews

The prospects for 1999 looked bright. The Arena tour with the Manics
had been met with a favourable response from the public who were awaiting the next single and album scheduled for release in late March and early
April.

Catatonia's last serious assault on the charts had been July 20th 1998,
with "Strange Glue". Despite the eight month gap between "Strange Glue"
and "Dead From The Waist Down", there was no reason to suppose that
the record buying public would desert the band. The music media still
loved Catatonia as evidenced by the awards nominations they had received.
However it must be noted that all the acclaim was centred on the first
seven months of 1998.

In January, *Melody Maker* published the results of their 1998 end of year
poll. Catatonia won the writer-voted awards for Best Album (*International
Velvet*) and Best Single ("Road Rage") along with the reader-voted award
for Best Single ("Road Rage"). This was a fine achievement for a song that
had only peaked at number 5 in the charts.

Cerys accepted the prizes and was clearly thrilled. "I think we deserve it
– not because I'm on it, but because of the songs. I'm really proud of the
songs."

She was also voted "Woman of the Year" and "Sexiest Woman of the Year" although she quickly pointed out that she was a lady and not a woman.

Her reaction to being Sexiest Woman was positive, confirming, "I do like sex a lot," then adding, "…when you love a band and you listen to their records and you think they're nice, that's the sexiest thing in the world. So if they vote for me, that means they think our music's good and that's no mean thing… 'cos it means they've got a bit of brain there. It's better than just voting with your cock."

For the Brit Awards 1998, Catatonia were nominated for Best Album (*International Velvet*), Best Band and Best Single ("Road Rage"). Catatonia were so confident they would win something on the night that Cerys had prepared eight acceptance speeches and was regularly clearing her throat. However, the tell-tale signs that they had not won rapidly became apparent. Band members were allowed to go to the toilet. If you are to win an award, it is claimed the minions refuse to let you leave the table for fear of missing the crucial announcement.

As the awards were presented, Cerys became increasingly incensed with the winners. "Belle and Sebastian – Best New Band according to Radio 1 listeners. Well I'm sorry, but that's not right is it?"

"And Natalie Imbruglia for Best International Newcomer! A fucking puppet! What about Lauryn Hill? This is bullshit. I don't want to win anything now."

I am afraid I put the kiss of death on Catatonia. I had three £25 doubles and a £25 treble on them winning their respective categories. I always bet on them – and it is not the most profitable exercise in the world. However, thanks to a telephone call shortly before the betting book was closed, from someone evidently in the know, I had a 55-to-1 win double on Belle and Sebastian and Ms Imbruglia. The information was confidential, because to be honest, I would not have touched either of these acts with your money.

Cerys tore up her acceptance speeches with an air of ceremony and laughingly said, "We was robbed."

And so was I, but at least I was able to recoup my losses.

If it is any consolation, an executive for Britannia Music stated in one of their periodical catalogues, "If I had a say in the Brits, Catatonia would be head and shoulders ahead in the Best British Album category, but I don't."

The day after the Brits, Catatonia commenced the 26-hour flight to New Zealand. Between February 20th and February 26th they played five gigs in New Zealand and Australia, starting at the Power Station in Auckland and finishing at the Prince of Wales, Melbourne.

They were not interested in in-flight movies and the travelling was eased by alcohol and Melatonin. A two-hour stop off at Hong Kong for refuelling failed to raise Cerys who had lost it. Generally she gets quite sick travelling – "aeroplane food and that – and we travel a lot".

Paul managed to buy a Chairman Mao fridge magnet in the tourist lounge before the rest of the band returned to the plane. He had enjoyed gigging with Sheffield band Pulp in 1998 and this purchase alone would have gained him honorary citizenship of the People's Republic of South Yorkshire.

When they disembarked in Auckland, Cerys admitted to feeling ill. Unknown to the band there were TV crews to film their arrival. As a result of the jet lag and alcohol they could not give a coherent interview. Cerys later admitted to being embarrassed by this, but in her defence she is not a great lover of air travel at the best of times, although she will confess to one advantage. "Airline socks are really good. I threw out all the others. I just collected everybody's socks on the plane."

During the tour it was mild, not too hot, but definitely not sock weather. However there was little chance to enjoy any sightseeing because of the amount of time spent on planes and at airports. Paul remarked that it would have been nice to have had more time there and to be able to drive around.

While they were in Melbourne, Cerys sought out some diversions and managed to indulge her passion for karaoke. None of the band members or crew eat Japanese cuisine so she spent a lot of time on her own in a Japanese restaurant. Having made friends with the sushi chef they took off to a local karaoke brothel.

Ignoring what went on behind the closed doors of this establishment in case it shocked her Celtic innocence, she managed to convince the patrons that she had a genuine love of karaoke and proceeded to enjoy herself by singing the night away.

At their final gig in Melbourne there was an audience of 900, many waving Welsh flags and sporting Welsh rugby shirts. Cerys' bad moods became more frequent and she had an onstage jibe at the American singer/poet Jewel, who was also playing in Melbourne. The signs of stress were beginning to show.

Q magazine had sent a journalist to cover the tour, and after the gig, Cerys, still sombre, said of Mark:

"With us it was always a love/hate thing anyway. Now it's mostly hate."

She added that no matter where the band are in the world, Mark will check his watch and comment that he should be back in Cardiff with the lads in the pub.

Mark readily admits to this and he, most of all, misses his home comforts. He comes across as a regular person who you could chat to in a pub or anywhere once he is comfortable in your company.

On one occasion he remembered he owed me a drink – this was after the band had been plying their trade overseas – yet he recalled that minor detail two months later.

After the interview the band met up with their old friends the Super Furry Animals who had, coincidentally, played a gig in the city the same night. Both bands were in the mood for celebration. They split into several groups and hit the clubs, Cerys claiming a huge desire to get pissed. She was also yearning to get home but dreading the 24-hour plane journey. It was after dawn when she returned, leaving her just time to pack. She was looking small and frail.

"I can't wait to get home. I'm desperate for a shag."

She was obviously tired and out of it. Presumably she was referring to a special shag she had in mind, from someone dear to her. For perhaps the first time in her career, she had either deliberately or inadvertently opened up slightly on her private life.

The return flight was to be even more of a problem to Cerys than she could have anticipated. "I put bleach in my eye by mistake. Specsavers are trying me out on all these new sorts of contact lenses and they gave me a new system because I've become a little bit lazy and they were worried about my eyes. I packed in a real hurry and took the wrong stuff, so I put bleach in my eyes. It was agony. It was so strong that my nose was going really badly and I was too ashamed to ask for help, because it would have looked really bad, y'know."

The jet travel had not helped matters, but it was beginning to look as though the heavy schedule of the past fifteen months or so was taking its toll on Cerys. Over the next few months, during interviews she was beginning to show distinct signs of being under pressure.

"You just want to tell everyone to fuck right off. I'm in a bad way right now. You haven't caught me at my best – sorry. I need to go off on my own for a while, see some sheep," she commented.

Whilst clearly loving the limelight and attention, equally clearly she needed some space. In the interview with *Q* magazine she dropped her guard on certain parts of her life. She even had a few caustic digs at Mark in the public domain.

Mark was not as unfortunate though as a certain kangaroo. As a souvenir of the tour, Cerys acquired a new purse bag made from a kangaroo's scrotum. She explained, "Aborigines used to carry them. They haven't got a seam, because they're shaped like a ball."

Some creatures, however, did have their equipment in working order, or at least it was hoped that they had. Whilst the group were in Australia, a zoo in Colwyn Bay, North Wales was trying to pair off two of its golden eagles that were named Tom Jones and Cerys Matthews.

"Maybe I'm contradicting everything I said in Australia, but I never wanted fame really. I just wanted to be a great singer. This life… it's not natural is it," she told Q magazine on her return from the Southern hemisphere. For a second she looked like she was about to cry. She doesn't, but she closes her eyes and keeps them closed.

"People have this idea of me being loud and brash and feisty," she continues, "but that is only half the time. There's a different side to me that people just don't see. I need a break from all this constant attention. I just want to go home. I want to go walking along the cliffs…"

Whether it was the result of the shag she'd been craving, or whether the cliff top walk had restored her passion for life, she was soon to bounce back, as frothy as ever.

"Dead From The Waist Down" had been chosen as the first single to be released from the album. Patricia Murphy, who had amongst other projects directed TV ads for Volvo, was given responsibility for the video. It was made over two days – March 4th and 5th.

The theme of the video was Cerys' idea, and it allowed her to fulfil her fantasy of playing a latter-day Dorothy in a *Wizard of Oz* setting. The scenery was a riot of colour. She encountered a problem with the bosses at Blanco Y Negro over their reluctance to pay the price of the corn to be used on the set.

For her character in the shoot, Cerys wore a plunging bodice that forced her bosoms to overflow to such an extent that the band were taking bets which one would fall out first. The corset had to be tightened while she was wearing it, thus causing any wind from her body to be expelled from her nether orifice – straight into the face of the man knelt behind her doing the tightening.

Cerys also got to roll in the hay with a hunk from the Gold Blend ads. Regarding kissing the hunk, the director called for a Hollywood kiss with no tongues or exchanges of bodily fluids, but this was Cerys she was talking to, and these guidelines were quickly forgotten and she admitted she acted, "like a tart. Absolute slapper."

Mark appeared dressed as a country bumpkin. He had a disaster with hair dye for the shoot. He should have been ash-blond but ended up a gingery colour, looking more like a thinking-man's Chris Evans than a mid-West oik.

Paul played a woodcutter, Owen was dressed as a blacksmith and pegged out on a washing line, while Aled was an orange skinned scarecrow with a sack on his head.

Also about this time, Cerys once again undertook work outside the band, getting involved in a film project called *Eagle's Claw*. The film featured several pop stars reciting humorous dialogue over a montage of martial arts footage. Cerys Matthews supplied the voice of Princess Koo, Tommy Scott (Space) was Master Chow, and Tim Wheeler (Ash) voiced Long Wang. *Eagle's Claw* premiered on MTV on March 4th.

Next on Catatonia's agenda was an eleven-gig Spring tour of medium sized venues to promote "Dead From The Waist Down" and showcase material from *Equally Cursed And Blessed*. The tour started at Derby Assembly Rooms on March 10th and concluded at Hereford Leisure Centre on March 24th. The support act were fellow Welsh band Big Leaves.

Since the spectre of being dropped by their label prior to the success of *International Velvet*, things had become remarkably upbeat in the Catatonia camp. Cerys was now enthusing about the improvements to the stage set. "We've got a lighting engineer. People are prepared to pay for our lights y'know. We're not gonna be dropped."

This is another simple yet warming facet of Catatonia. They appreciate what they have achieved and they like to share that with anyone who will listen.

The tour had been referred to by several music journos as a crossover tour. This appeared to be jargonistic bollocks. Catatonia did not need to tour to achieve the so-called "crossover". They had already well and truly arrived.

I was looking forward to this outing as I could get to six of the gigs. Five were easy to travel to; Sheffield, Derby, Wolverhampton, Manchester and Leeds. The sixth one at Hereford was a little more awkward, but I always like to be at the last gig of a Catatonia tour.

In the meantime I had also been telephoning various housing agencies in the Cardiff area to secure some reasonable accommodation. Consequently, within a few weeks of the tour finishing, I would be moving to Wales on a permanent basis to continue my passion of working with unsigned bands.

Prior to the first gig, *Melody Maker* offered its readers a vivid portrait of Catatonia's front-woman. "Luckily, Cerys is normal life through and through. She drinks, swears, listens to Radio 2 while doing the washing up, enjoys sex, shouts along to Frank Sinatra at last orders; all the stuff people know and understand. She's every woman, common and proud."

The gig itself was good but not exceptional. A typical first night. The media were focussed on this gig, and indeed the tour. Because of the enormity of the band's success and the elevation to major celebrity status of their singer in 1998, seldom has a tour of venues of this size aroused so much interest. What was the fascination?

Were Catatonia, about to soar out of the solar system?

Were they a flash in the pan?

Was the singer so exceptionally gifted?

Would she fall on her arse?

It was probably a combination of all these. While bemoaning that "the venue itself had all the cheery ambience of a bus station," *The Observer* also commented, "The Derby show was promising… Catatonia played six new songs, all of which were warmly received by the uncommonly tough crowd."

The Observer's critic also recounted Cerys' introduction to "Mulder and Scully": "'You'll have to help me with this one – I don't like singing it,' before launching into it with all the passion and excitement of a housewife forced to hang out someone else's washing. Clearly, Catatonia's songwriting heart lay elsewhere. The question was, would the public at large follow them?" (Earlier in the year, Cerys had been none too happy about having to sing the hit song in Australia. She felt obligated to perform it because it was featured on the advertisements for their concerts.)

After the Derby concert Steve Lamacq said, "'She's a Millionaire' was one of the best tracks tonight. You always wait for that new, sassy Catatonia song, and that sounds like it's the one." He welcomed the blend of new songs and old favourites and mentioned Cerys' wine swigging exploits. "This is the start of the crossover," he added, "because there are a lot of people with grey hair and taches here." It was obvious, however, that the original fans were still present; on this tour I was to see people I had met over the years in Amsterdam, Copenhagen, Brussels, Swansea, Liverpool, Norwich, Aberystwyth, Newport, Llanelwedd and so on.

Following the Wolverhampton gig, Catatonia played the Sheffield Octagon on March 12th. Cerys took to the stage drinking from a huge bottle of Liebfraumilch and smoking a cigarette, seemingly without a care in the world. She took two swigs from the bottle, then noticed that the crew had fixed a small shelf on the mic stand for her wine. She turned to the band and started laughing, before asking the audience, "Did any of you go to that gig in that big shed (Sheffield Arena) in December? That was our worst fucking gig ever. Tonight, we'll try and make up for it."

And they did.

Audience and band clearly enjoyed each other. Waves of appreciation and emotion flowing both ways. Robbie Williams' phoney niece was mentioned, with Cerys reassuring us that, "With Catatonia, you get the truth."

At the end of the gig the applause was long and deafening, prompting Cerys to announce, "I haven't enjoyed myself as much for a long time. Thank you."

The lights went out and there were chants of "More" and "Cerys". Eventually, the faintest of spotlights came on, and a barely distinguishable figure was shuffling across the stage. He looked quizzically at the audience.

"What do you want?" he enquired.

"Cerys" shouted the 1,200 in unison for a good few minutes.

Then the lights came on at the same time as the band took to the stage. The lonely figure had been Aled, and he had spoken on stage! Fame must have gone to his head.

A few songs into the encore and the band made to leave after doing their normal quota.

"My band are leaving me. Do you want any more?" Cerys shouted, whilst stamping her foot in the direction of the disappearing musicians.

We got two more songs.

Afterwards, the packed crowd moved slowly towards the main exit. I could not feel the ground with my feet. It was a weird sensation. As soon as we hit the marble floor at the top of the stairs outside of the hall, I paused, shook one leg and immediately went arse-over-tit down the entire flight of steps. During the concert, two pint-sized, plastic beer containers had slid over the length of my trainers without me noticing. Such is the joy of going to gigs.

A couple of days later and the group were in Newcastle. Cerys was delighted to find herself staying in the same hotel as Monica Lewinsky, who was on a book promotion tour. But, despite hanging around lifts and hotel bars, Cerys never did get to meet Ms Lewinsky. Apparently, Cerys was "gutted" not to have pressed the flesh – especially as Mark had put Monica (plus five) on the guest list for that night's gig. Lewinsky, apparently, stayed in to wash her hair.

This was not wasted on *Melody Maker*'s ascerbic ficticious columnist, Mr Agreeable, who commented, "Oh! At fucking last. The woman who abused sex appeal to get a job, is found in the same hotel as the woman who sucked off Bill Clinton. And we were all wondering how Catatonia managed to stay signed to Warners for so fucking long. Lord above, can you imagine these two getting together. One with a knob tied round her throat, and the other one... Fuck me!"

Towards the end of the tour, Cerys picked up a bad chest infection and began to look exhausted and depressed. In addition to the gigging so far that year, she had been all over London following her hectic schedule, giving interview after interview. No wonder she was getting 'weirded out'.

Publicly she was dismissive of the strain. "Every band has its shelf life. We're all aware of that. Things are good for us at the moment, so we're not about to ease up. Why would we? Real life's too dull in comparison."

Cerys' valiant solo attempt at emptying the European wine lake and friendly audience interaction had become the norm for this tour. The last gig was at Hereford Leisure Centre on March 24th. For whatever reason, Cerys was confused on the night. "Thanks for coming. Hey it's great to be back in Wales." This was very gracious, but it came as a culture shock to many in the 2,000 strong audience who, like me, were under the assumption that they were in England. At the band's end of tour party in an upstairs bar at the Leisure Centre, she told friends, "I could have sworn we were in Wales."

Never one to shun the limelight herself, Cerys had always thrown a protective veil over her romances and flings with the opposite sex. Being so often in London makes it harder to protect your privacy.

The Sun broke the news. "Cerys is wooed by producer," stating that, "Catatonia singer Cerys Matthews is dating the band's producer Tommy D. The Welsh babe tried desperately to keep her romance under wraps, but friends let it slip. One pal says, 'It's very early days, but they've been friends a long time. They have worked together for ages and their friendship has blossomed into something a bit more special.'"

With the tabloids, it is always "one pal" and they never get identified. Unless Cerys had wanted the story leaking, then no pal of hers would have spilled the beans. The posse are too loyal.

True fans of Catatonia, and there are many, were not that interested in such tabloid speculation. They just love the music and the people in the band, and at this time were eagerly awaiting their next release rather than an exposé of the singer's love life.

An advance press release for the new single, "Dead From The Waist Down" announced, "It's an understated ballad, drenched in strings and dripping with sadness. It's by far the most dainty track Cerys and Co have penned, so if you've been immune to their charms thus far, your time may well be up."

Another commentator stated, "A luscious, irresistibly smoochy ballad that comes laden with strings, strings and more strings. Number 1 for several weeks if there's any justice in the world."

There wasn't.

Meanwhile, the *New Musical Express* gave an advance review of the new album *Equally Cursed and Blessed.* "Catatonia really are flying up and away with the pop fairies. Careering from Celtic tinklings, to trip-hopping trinkets. Today, Catatonia's new songwriting angles appear to be that the Monarchy is very shit, London is extremely shit and love is a bit shit, but not all the time."

Staying with the *New Musical Express*, the issue for week ending March 27th featured an interview with the band taken at the time of the video shoot for "Dead From The Waist Down". The interviewer touched on the former relationship between Cerys and Mark, which seemed to genuinely hurt Cerys.

Eventually, she described how she had become more positive with time and had striven to get over it, saying, "The best thing that ever happened to me was having my heart broken."

Naturally enough, Cerys featured on the front cover, on a garden swing, wearing the dress featured in the video, scowling at the camera. *The Sun* saw fit to criticise her for "ruining the look". They were obviously ignorant of Cerys' approach to posing for pictures. "If someone wants to take pictures of me, I want them to take pictures of me looking ridiculous."

On March 26th, "Dead From the Waist Down" was aired on *TFI Friday* before the single was released on March 29th. It was issued in CD, 7" vinyl, and cassette form. B-sides on the CD were "Bad, Bad Boy" and "Branding a Mountain." Its highest chart position was number 7.

Cerys thought very highly of the song and rated "Dead From The Waist Down" equal with "Do You Believe In Me" as the best Catatonia song, stating it was the closest they'd ever come to a Pacific Ocean vibe. In her opinion it was a classy yet beautiful song that made you feel warm inside. It was well within her vocal range and not as demanding to sing as "Mulder and Scully" and "Road Rage".

The song was seen as the flagship of the album and was therefore designated to be the first single. However, with its summery vibe, it was probably released at the wrong time of year. We Brits are creatures of habit, and we relate songs about the weather to the current climate. "The sun is shining… etc." The only record to have had a worse release date in 1999 was the English Cricket Team's world cup song – which came out the day after they had been eliminated.

June would have been a better release date because we would have either been basking in the sun, or if the weather was inclement we would have been dreaming of better days, and this is the perfect song for either situation. True pop standards are rare, but they stand the test of time, so watch out for someone doing a cover version in a few years.

There were busy times ahead for the band, April 3rd saw them play the Amsterdam *London Calling Festival* again, followed on April 5th with Live from Kentish Town Forum on Radio 1 to conclude Steve Lamacq's *Live In London* event. It was also Radio 1 Catatonia day.

Cerys' accent was more pronounced than usual on the radio show indicating she had recently visited West Wales. In fact, she'd "just got back from a week in Pembrokeshire with the family. I can relax there and if I so much as begin to behave like a pop princess, they would laugh me out of town."

Through the success of Catatonia she had rapidly become one of the most sought after subjects by the media. A combination of being highly photogenic, an effervescent personality, a love of being in the limelight and an opinion on most things, made her a natural target.

In one interview, she had already admitted that she would happily take the lead in posing naked, if the price was right. It would be no way connected with selling her music but it would put some money in her bank account.

Eventually, an editor took the initiative. The men's magazine *FHM* featured Cerys in its May issue. She appeared on the front cover, provocatively but tastefully clad in a PVC suit. Cerys admitted, "I think it surprised a lot of people, particularly the band. Mark said to me, 'Why are you in that soft porn thing?'"

In fact the photographs had been well thought out and there were no tit, bum, or knicker shots. (Surprising for the latter, since she has a reputation for deliberately flashing them during publicity shoots.) Being appreciative of the female form, she had no qualms about showing hers. She met the editor of *FHM*, they got on well and she decided to go for it. On publication, feminists wrote letters of complaint to the music media alleging it was degrading for women to do this sort of thing.

"It was my decision," she stressed. "Did I subvert it? I don't think I did bugger all." Cerys did not need to do it to get noticed, nor is she the sort of person to do things she doesn't want to.

The album *Equally Cursed and Blessed* was released on April 12th, the track list being, "Dead From The Waist Down", "Londinium", "Postscript", "She's A Millionaire", "Storm The Palace", "Karaoke Queen", "Bulimic Beats", "Valerian", "Shoot The Messenger", "Nothing Hurts", "Dazed Beautiful and Bruised".

It went straight to number 1 in the album charts selling more than 60,000 copies in the first week. Woolworths ran a promotion where they offered *Way Beyond Blue* as "a perfect partner" at a reduced price (£4.99) to purchasers of the new album. This assisted *Way Beyond Blue* to chart at number 32 and with *International Velvet* at number 36, Catatonia had the distinction of having three albums in the top 40. It was their second number 1 album in less than a year.

Originally, Mark had wanted to put a chessboard on the cover of the album, but Cerys wanted prams. Neither achieved their objective. In the end it featured a fox and chicken, supposedly symbolic of good and evil.

Almost as much time seemed to have been spent on finding a title for the new album as recording it. The earliest working title in autumn 1998 was 'Catatonia Are Shit.' Obviously aimed at that part of the market they had not yet reached – the Darby and Joan, tea and cucumber sandwiches on the lawn set in Cheltenham.

Aled enlighteningly explained, "Yeah! But now we have a better title than that one – 'Catatonia Are Really Shit.'"

In the end, *Equally Cursed and Blessed* was chosen by Mark and came from the lyrics to "She's A Millionaire".

Maxim magazine favourably reviewed the album. "Cerys is touched by a little Celtic magic and this album is more blessed than cursed. Despite impending global mega-stardom, the band still bursts with bubbly energy and confidence."

Melody Maker was also impressed; "This really is Sweet Catatonia. This is a record which sounds like nobody else matters, like Catatonia are the only band in the world... here is a band actually enjoying themselves."

Strangely, *New Musical Express*, who had enthusiastically previewed the album a few weeks before were not impressed. "Around half of *Equally Cursed and Blessed* then is fairly insipid, orchestral indie pop fluff, as harmless and cutesy-pie soft as a baby seal crying out for a right good culling..."

People who subscribe to both *Melody Maker* and *New Musical Express* would find themselves very confused, as the respective reviews were literally, equally cursed and blessed.

Discussing some of the album tracks, Mark described the lyrics of "Storm The Palace" as being about the dear old Queen's house – suggesting new and different uses for the building. It has been used very effectively for starting off their gigs, but is also a song that the BBC seem to have problems with. This was probably why it was not released as a single.

Cerys wrote "Bulimic Beats" which, unlike Catatonia's other material, is based on actual personal experience as she suffered from bulimia at one time in her life. "A lot of girls have eating disorders, I, myself included. It's not that uncommon, is it?" she admits. "So I think you have to have humour about it."

Cerys' experience with bulimia occurred like quite a few other things, from being at a loose end. She explains, "it is boredom, and the lack of a mother around to give you a good slap."

The album, possibly as a result of its diversity, appealed to a variety of tastes. One critic ventured to suggest that "Cerys has never sounded better than on 'Valerian'". The song goes down well in continental Europe where fans have taken it to heart.

"Londinium" proclaims "tourism is congestion". Mark fails to see the point in tourists flocking to London when most of them have seen it on the television. There is an in-band joke in the lyrics of the song. Mark was getting very bored with Cerys frequently talking about sushi and always wanting to go to a sushi bar. So he penned the lines, "Sushi bars, wet fish / It just sucks" to poke fun at Cerys knowing that she would have to sing them.

Criticism was levelled at Catatonia from a section of the music press concerning the party they threw at the Teatro restaurant on Shaftesbury

Avenue to launch the album. They were compared to the Fun Loving Criminals who had also recently celebrated an album release.

It contrasted the two guest lists. The Fun Loving Criminals stuck with their old crew whilst Catatonia's launch was full of "multi-yachted rock bloaters". It went on to mention that Catatonia locked themselves in the VIP room at the back and refused to come out and talk to anybody. (Catatonia did not have control over who was invited and probably chose to mix with those people they felt most comfortable with.)

"Dispatches from behind the divine red rope, however, brought tales of Cerys getting so plastered, she almost ended up breaking her neck while teaching Tom Jones how to break dance. But then again we always suspected she was a little dead from the neck up," the critic bitchily concluded.

The album release fuelled the interest of the press and the *Daily Telegraph* ran an interview with Cerys in which she outlined her previous weeks' hectic activities.

"April 8th Catatonia recorded *Top Of The Pops*. 9th played *TFI Friday*. Saturday 10th Cerys took the 'Stretch Limo to my parent's house to celebrate [her birthday] with friends and family; then a minibus picking up whoever could stand on Sunday morning [11th] to take us to watch a rugby international [at Wembley].'

Sunday night 'we were partying with the Welsh rugby team.' Monday night [12th] 'we had the launch party for the album.' Tuesday night 'we had something else going on'. Wednesday night [14th] 'I went to a fashion show at the Planetarium.' Thursday [15th] 'flew to Germany with my brother to show him this bar in Hamburg.'

'Apart from that, nothing much happened really.'"

I was probably just as busy chasing up accommodation in Cardiff, which is not a straightforward thing to do from Sheffield. My best friend Garry knew how much passion I had for music and Wales and could readily understand how frustrated I was becoming with the situation. So he suggested that the thing to do was for him to drive me down and we would look at some places and hopefully chose one. This we did. In less than a month I would make the permanent move that had been so painstakingly obvious for the past few years.

Having launched the album, a relatively quiet period followed before the band played on the *Later With Jools Holland* programme on April 23rd, in which Cerys was also interviewed by the man himself. Next day, April 24th, Cerys and Owen played an unplugged slot on Johnnie Walker's BBC

Radio 2 show. These duets were now becoming another part of the band's armory, and enhanced radio interviews with acoustic arrangements of the fans' favourites.

It is generally a sign that you have arrived if people make fun of you on established TV shows and that honour was to befall Catatonia. Over the May Bank Holiday, French and Saunders did a comedy version of the "Mulder and Scully" video, calling the song "Cymru Pride", with Dawn French playing Cerys, knocking back the booze, dragging on a cig, singing "Don't mess with me, I'm a working class Taffy". A spokeswoman for the BBC said, "Dawn and Jennifer were huge fans of Catatonia and that they go for whoever they are listening to at the time. If French and Saunders do make fun of people, it means they are a household name, otherwise there would be no point doing it."

Catatonia missed the sketch first time round as they were preparing to headline the Heineken Green Energy Festival on May 2nd/3rd at Belfast Botanical Gardens and Dublin Castle. They were supported by The Cardigans and Gay Dad. At these gigs, Cerys hung around with Gay Dad's Cliff Jones. Touched by a generous gift of vodka from Cerys, Cliff presented her with his black sequined waistcoat, which she wore on stage at both gigs.

For the early part of 1999 the frantic pace had continued for Catatonia. They had achieved another number 1 album, even though *Equally Cursed and Blessed* seemed destined not to sell as many copies as *International Velvet*. It was a very hard act to follow. What was disappointing was the poor chart showing of "Dead From The Waist Down". It only made number 7.

Could it be that *The Observer* had been right to query whether the public at large would follow the change of songwriting direction? Certainly there were disconcerting signs that some of the media coverage was now becoming hostile. With Cerys seemingly always available for promotional work and publicity, both on the group's behalf and her own, there was an increased risk of her vulnerability being exploited.

They had been given no time out to prepare a new stage set, which was seemingly causing frustration, but worst of all was the indication that the hectic work schedule, combined with her hedonistic lifestyle, were taking their toll on Cerys. Despite the warnings there was no sign of anyone taking their foot off the pedal. It worried me that Cerys could be heading down the road leading to a nervous breakdown or mental and physical exhaustion. A road I was all too familiar with.

SUSHI BARS WET FISH

I like doing 'Do You Believe In Me', but not often because it's the kind of song you just don't want to sing too many times.

Cerys Matthews

Organisers of festivals and ceremonies were more than keen to get Catatonia on their bills. As a result of their recent successes more prestigious slots had been offered and played. However, the band themselves had embarked on a brave venture and were instrumental in organising three high profile concerts to take place in their native Wales in May. These were to be called *The Home Internationals*.

Other UK gigs would be limited, but of an exceptional nature. Musically, the growing concern was the relatively poor showing in the singles charts, but on a personal level many wondered how long the band could keep up their punishing schedule.

1999 was a good time to be in Catatonia and a good time to be in Wales with the prospect of the formation of the Welsh Assembly, the Rugby World Cup Finals, and five major pop events. There were the three Catatonia *Home International Concerts*, the Stereophonics at Morfa Stadium, Swansea and the Manic Street Preachers at the Millennium Stadium on Millennium Eve.

For the third Catatonia *Home International Concert,* Ian Brown confirmed that he had received a personal invite from Cerys to be the special guest at Margam Park. He said, "Cerys had been told I'd received a letter about it in jail, saying that she wanted me to play, but I hadn't. I'd only heard of the shows the same day that I met her. That's the one reason I'm doing it – it felt right."

"I'm playing out of respect for Cerys and Catatonia. Putting on a show for 30,000 fans in your home area is something I can relate to. I hope it's a red hot, sunny day. It's gonna be a thriller."

Saturday May 8th was a personal landmark for me. I moved to Cardiff to work with up-and-coming bands and to try to put something back into music. After all, one way or another, I have had a lot out of it. I was filled with immense pride to have a permanent Welsh address at long last.

Then the unexpected... Apparently, Catatonia were playing a secret lunchtime concert at the London Astoria on the same day. The music press stated, "Catatonia treated a handful of their keenest fans to an exclusive, free lunchtime gig. The majority of the tickets were given as prizes by an unofficial Catatonia website, the rest given out to winners of an XFM radio competition. I considered that the method of the ticket allocation was poorly thought-out. There had to be a better way, although I admit none came to mind.

Adam Shutes, who runs the website, did tell me later that he was only given the final go ahead to run the competition for tickets some nine days before the concert, but as my computer had been boxed up for some time pending the move I missed the announcements.

The concert was an hour-long effort for the Fuji TV show, starting at two in the afternoon to fit in with a live satellite hook up with Japan. The entire set, apart from the encores, was broadcast and included "Storm The Palace" so it was probable that the impartial BBC would not be screening it live. Cerys, resplendent in a pink sequined dress, with a protruding purple Wonderbra, compared the early start to being like a junior school disco.

During "She's a Millionaire," Cerys was pelted with dozens of tampons. This was becoming a regular feature now, inspired by the line "Should be getting her tampons free". (Watch out for Cerys writing a new song with the lyrics, "should be getting her diamonds free.") An alien clad in a Welsh flag and a cotton wool sheep were also propelled towards the stage.

This gig was Catatonia's first broadcast to Japan, and heralded their inaugural visit to the islands to appear at the Fuji festival the following August. Cerys had a long-held fascination for Japan and all things Japanese, especially the food, and was eagerly looking forward to the visit.

Two days later, the band was gigging again in London. MTV had scheduled a series of concerts under the banner "Five Night Stand" to be held at London's Shepherds Bush Empire and shown at a later date.

Soon the billboards were proclaiming, "Due To Huge Popular Demand" – an extra night had been included to feature Catatonia who played on May 10th. "Special guests" for the show were Puressence, with whom the band had toured a few years earlier, and Belgian band dEUS.

Catatonia were scheduled to appear two days after my move and I was still settling in to my new environment, but that could wait. I had learned of the gig on teletext some weeks earlier and contacted the theatre who knew nothing about it. I telephoned a fellow fan in London, who went to the theatre, paid for the as yet unprinted ticket and obtained a receipt, which would be exchanged on the day for a ticket. There is a way round everything.

I arrived at my hotel about a quarter of a mile from the gig. When I opened the door to my room and there were clothes and luggage on the bed. I went to reception to report this. The manager assumed I was a loon and came up to the room. It was 2 pm.

"I told him to be out by 12 o'clock." he raged.

He then opened the window and threw all the guy's belongings into the main road below. (Obviously another Basil Fawlty.)

On stage Cerys, glistening in pink sequins, was swigging champagne from a bottle. She swung her mic around in her holster/handbag, and was gurgling about being late to arrive because, "Our train hit a cow. Well, half a cow it is now."

The gig went well, but as with all of these TV concerts, it seemed a bit like a clockwork event. The atmosphere more than made up for it. At times the stage reminded me of the set for Marlene Dietrich's *The Blue Angel*.

The next day I returned to Cardiff to start my new life and was shortly approached by Flipside, one of the city's best young bands, asking if I could help them. I was deeply flattered. The first gig I got them was supporting Gorky's Zygotic Mynci at The Attic, Cheltenham.

I needed a bit of time to focus on the music scene in South Wales and to give a fair bit of attention to the bands I was meeting. This meant I had to make certain decisions. The pop fans of Britain then finally heard the news that they had waited several years for. I was not planning to attend Glastonbury 1999.

"Let's run a coach trip!" seemed to be the mass response. People assumed because I was not going, then the weather would be fine. Typically, it was.

It was also at this time that I first managed to talk to some of the band members and their friends on a social basis. My main concern was not to encroach on their privacy. Since then our paths have crossed on numerous occasions. Off stage they are exactly how I had imagined, my experiences have confirmed them to be friendly and helpful. Yet, even so, I know I could not have spoken to them earlier given the personal battle I was fighting.

Meanwhile, over the pond, other things were on the immediate horizon for Catatonia. There was a Canadian launch for *Equally Cursed and Blessed* on May 11th, released on Blanco Y Negro and distributed by Warner Music Canada. It was a case of the right hand not knowing what the left hand was doing, in light of what later transpired. The group, however, had bigger fish to fry back home.

They presented their breathtaking venture under the banner *The Home Internationals,* staging two concerts at Llangollen Eisteddfod International Arena on May 22nd and 23rd to be followed by a concert at Margam Park, Port Talbot a week later on May 29th. The events bore the Catatonia trademark, from choice of support acts to planning security.

A trailer for the concerts boasted "Supersized brace of gigs for the band who like to wear a bindi 'n' bandana two-piece while swearing like lords and drinking enough brandy to float a pocket cruiser."

Previewing the first of these concerts in North Wales, a music journalist offered this advice. "Don't panic if you're planning on stopping over for the night. As an around-the-year holiday destination (Llangollen), you shouldn't struggle for a cheap place to lay your head."

Taking his advice, I decided not to telephone Llangollen Tourist Information until the Thursday before the gig.

"I'm sorry sir," was the reply, "there's no accommodation available this weekend. There's a pop concert on."

"Really?" I said. "Anybody good?"

"The Welsh band Catatonia," the lady informed me.

"Can't be anything special. I've never heard of them." I then sweet-talked her for over five minutes and she said she would call me back if anything turned up.

Sure enough, she was as good as her word. A man in the town was converting a building into a hostel and he had a vacancy, which I very gratefully accepted. Welsh hospitality is amazing. If Mary and Joseph had been going to Llangollen 2,000 years ago then they would not have had to rough it in a stable.

The band gave a press conference before the Llangollen gigs. They were asked about their views on the newly elected Welsh Assembly and whether as a band they could influence Welsh politics.

The press coverage was following the usual pattern through the career of a band. At stage one, newspapers are interested in the music and any interesting adventures that may have occurred in their early days. Stage two, when the band is successful, their opinions on a wide range of subjects are sought. The third phase is not so pleasant. This is when the press, generally certain tabloids, seem intent on destroying the image of the band that they themselves had helped to create. Progressing from one to three, the standard of journalism and the adherence to the truth tends to decline rapidly. There is an element of cat and mouse in all this, as some artists use the press unashamedly to promote their careers but forget that they are living in a goldfish bowl. Catatonia had now reached stage two.

The band then confirmed that they would not be playing at Cardiff's Millennium Stadium on Millennium Eve. It was stated that they had pulled out of supporting the Manic Street Preachers, but apparently they were never officially approached. They have never worked on New Year's Eve, so why now?

Owen said, "We're not doing the Millennium Stadium gig on New Year's Eve, because I can't think of a place more horrible to be in than a freezing cold, miserable and wet rugby stadium."

Later, Tom Shorey, Commercial and Sales Director of Millennium Stadium PLC said, "Catatonia obviously do not know that the stadium has a roof."

As the first band to play there at the opening ceremony of the Rugby World Cup, presumably they were aware of this. With 80% of them resident in Cardiff they saw it being built and were subjected to the publicity, as was everybody else who lived there.

The original capacity for Llangollen was 4,500 but extra marquees were added to accommodate a further 1,500. Cerys explained that the band had chosen Llangollen for the two shows because it was important to play North Wales as well as Margam Park in the South.

"North Wales was the first place we ever encountered people who sang along with our songs. Even the Welsh words to "International Velvet", added Owen.

The concert at Llangollen was the first time Cerys had been there, and she reaffirmed one of her early dreams. "I wanted to marry a farmer." This pushed Aled into action. "That's why we're playing in Llangollen then."

On the Friday night, one of the local football teams had won a vital game that secured them promotion. Naturally, they were out celebrating. Cerys bumped into them and joined in with the partying and singsong, She loved the evening and planned to find a bar and have another singsong when the gigs were over.

On the Saturday, in the arena itself, rumours were flying around that the band had been on stage in the morning to check things out, and that Cerys was so far out of it that she had to be sent back to the hotel to recover. Without these rumours it would not be a Catatonia gig, but they are so predictable that you wonder if the same person starts them all off.

Meanwhile, for some of the artists, the Saturday afternoon was spent in the comfort of the Llangollen Hands Hotel prior to going on stage. Mark watched the F.A. Cup Final, as his beloved Manchester United were playing. He predicted the result would be 3–0 to Manchester United, with Scholes scoring first. It finished up at 2–0 but Mark was delighted. When the match was over, Catatonia sent the support bands bottles of champagne with a note that read, "2–0. Next stop Barcelona! Thanks from Catatonia." Aled was not so lucky. He had just been hammered at table tennis by Richard Parfitt (ex-60 ft Dolls).

Later, across at the concert, Cerys was surrounded by other people's babies and howled, "God! All these men, and their babies. I'm barren."

She then took her family downstairs to dance to Gorky's Zygotic Mynci, but then had to stop them pirouetting across the stage.

"It's mad having all our parents here. When they're let outside the house they can be madder and louder and more drunk that anyone from the younger generation. It's 'cos they don't get out much. They don't get to go to many rock concerts. They started a conga at a Manics gig last year."

Catatonia often entertain family and friends after concerts, which sees groups of kids and middle-aged men and women joining in the fun. Familial bliss is very much part of the band. The essence of their genius is how they combine boozing, bad behaviour, genuinely populist tastes and a wash of human warmth.

Backstage, before going on, Mark nudged Cerys and said, "Oh Cerys. This could be legendary. In between songs, you've gotta just talk in Welsh."

She did. It was.

At the Saturday gig there was a tremendous atmosphere of patriotic fervour. Cerys frequently addressed the audience in Welsh, and after she had thanked the support bands, a heckler shouted, "What?"

"Don't you understand," she laughed, "I said they were bollocks."

During the set, Cerys turned to Mark, at the start of a song that she had cocked up, and said, "I'm sorry Mark, I was waiting for the backing singers."

This was the first time in what seemed like ages that I had heard Cerys address Mark by name on stage.

At the end of the gig, as they were about to leave the stage (prior to returning for the encore) Cerys announced, "This is a first for us. Our very own festival."

The pause between the show and the encore was to provide a very moving moment for me. The tent was in darkness. Some lighter flames provided a series of miniature beacons. Then, a few Welsh voices started singing "Land of My Fathers" in their native tongue, (Mae Hen Wlad Fy Nhadau). More and more people joined in, and they were all in key. The hairs on the back of my neck rose, a lump came to my throat and tears rolled from my eyes. Thank God Cerys and harpist Elinor Bennett came on to render "Bulimic Beats", otherwise I would have completely lost it.

The finale was electric as Cerys danced with a Welsh flag, thumped her chest with pride and led every person in the pavilion through "International Velvet". As always, this Englishman, this plastic Taff, was as proud as anyone there, when he joined in with, "Everyday, when I wake up, I thank the Lord I'm Welsh."

Later, in typical fashion back at their hotel, Catatonia celebrated until dawn. Cerys, allegedly, was still singing in a church doorway as the sun rose.

The beer tent was a less happy memory. It worked on the principle that you pre-paid for your drinks – warm beer, lager, cider, or probably sheep piss – by obtaining tickets for £2.50 which were exchanged for a drink. I was told that the bar would be open until 10.30pm. After the concert, I went to the bar at 10.15pm to find it long since shut. Predictably, the tickets were non-transferable and non-refundable.

I then went into a pub in Llangollen itself to grab a few late pints. Though Catatonia were playing the next day, I had chosen to give that one a miss and return to Cardiff. I find gigs never have the same atmosphere on a Sunday.

In the pub a group of us were chatting about the concert and other things. We were a motley crew, but there was one guy who was from Oswestry who was bugging everyone. The topic under discussion was "favourite Catatonia song." Oswestry Man interrupted the flow, looked me in the eye and said, "Oi! Have you shagged Cerys?"

For once in my life, I was speechless.

The answer obviously is no. But I just couldn't work out where he was coming from, or why he had asked me. (I was also still trying to work out why I was upset that I had been duped out of two pints of piss at the arena.)

It was the last question I had expected being asked of anyone. The conversation had been about music and the band members in general, not as individuals. Gradually the chat returned to something like normality, but I was still puzzled about the motives of Oswestry Man.

While we were drinking our last pint, he struck again, as he wanted to know what everyone's favourite Cerys fantasy was. To me a fantasy, is just that and should be kept personal, no matter what it is. Strangely enough the punters were falling for it and fuelling Oswestry Man's dreams. I tried to drift away. I did not want to hear this crap. Oswestry Man spotted me, "What's your fantasy, Yorky?" Though I say it myself, one of my strong points is being able to think on my feet.

"Oh. That's easy," I replied. "When you get older, like myself, some things take a little longer, but they are a lot better and you and your partner get total pleasure."

"On one Sunday in December," I continued," I would take her to some of the villages on the outskirts of Sheffield. Namely, Worrall, Oughtibridge, Dungworth and Bolsterstone. These places have loads of local Christmas Carols that you will not hear elsewhere. They have been passed down from generation to generation. The best time to hear them sung is in the village pubs on the Sunday lunchtimes immediately leading up to Christmas. The pubs are packed, and everybody joins in. The younger generation learning from the old. All of them singing unaccompanied. There is no friendlier atmosphere. It just transcends time with a majesty all of its own. That would put a smile on her face and give Cerys longer lasting pleasure than what you've all been on about."

They gave me strange looks. I drank up my pint and left.

The next morning after an early breakfast, I set off to catch the bus to Wrexham where I was to board the train home. Llangollen was dead and the bus was not due for over four hours. It had not seemed like a long journey on the way in and it was a pleasant morning, so I thought I would walk and enjoy the scenery. About sixteen miles later, I arrived at Wrexham utterly knackered. As a result of the sun and the hedgerows, a collection of insects and flies were stuck on my face and head. I glanced in a mirror – I looked like a busted Eccles cake.

While this was happening to a wrecked English exile, Catatonia would still be getting over the excesses of the previous night.

It was Sunday afternoon and Owen explained, "We've tried to get a sense of occasion going. Last summer after *International Velvet* did well, there was a load of pressure on us to do a big gig and announce we'd arrived. All of this was booked six months ago, well before the album *Equally Cursed and Blessed* came out. We'd have been in big trouble if that had bombed wouldn't we? 'Egg on face' wouldn't have come close."

At 4pm, Cerys got out of bed, groaned, and promptly returned to her slumbers. A couple of hours later she finally surfaced, "Oh. Did I really speak just Welsh?" she blushed. "Oh shit. Really? God knows what I said. It was probably being on the hallowed turf of an Eisteddfod Royal Pavilion. You can't speak anything else."

Wednesday May 26th was the day that the Welsh Assembly was officially inaugurated. The band had been invited but declined to make an appearance at the *Voices of the Nation Show* in Cardiff Bay because they were too busy with the *Home Internationals* concerts.

One journalist wrote, "The live TV concert to celebrate the opening of the Welsh Assembly was an unmitigated disaster. Catatonia's "International Velvet" should have been a rousing all-star finale, but instead it was unbelievably embarrassing for Wales.

Catatonia had given the BBC permission to use the anthem. Instead TV viewers saw Bonnie Tyler, Shakin' Stevens, Max Boyce, Tom Jones, Mike Peters, Charlotte Church and others singing "Everyday when I wake up, I thank the Lord I'm Welsh", while the live open-air audience was unable to hear a thing over the sound of the fireworks. So the anthem that was intentionally written as a piss-take, finally succeeded in its objective.

It was turning out to be quite a hectic week for Catatonia. The band had been nominated for an Ivor Novello award for Best Contemporary Song.

For anyone who knows anything about music "Road Rage" appeared to have little competition from the other nominations. It had already won several similar awards that had been decided by knowledgeable people, i.e. the record buying public and the music press. For those who know nothing about music then apply for a job as an adjudicator for Best Contemporary Song, and you will be in good company.

The Awards were presented at Grosvenor House on London's Park Lane, on May 27th and, as you would expect, there were the penguin-suits and their blue-rinse female companions in abundance. You know – those people you see at the Horse of the Year Show, Henley Regatta, Royal Ascot and the Splott Car Boot social scene.

As a demonstration of their champagne-soaked musical knowledge and caviar fattened expertise, the award went to "Here's Where The Story Ends" by Tin Tin Out. Presumably, the adjudicators were oblivious to the fact that the winning entry was a cover version of a nine-year-old Sundays song. Hardly contemporary.

"Road Rage" is regularly played on juke boxes all over the country and people love to sing along. The song is synonymous with Catatonia; the feel-good factor and the spirit of 1998. It is already a pop classic, and what of "Here's Where The Story Ends"?

Cerys was overheard in the ladies toilet (not by me) expressing her disappointment. The air turned blue as she cursed almost everybody involved with the adjudication. She respects the works of her fellow countryman, Cardiff-born Ivor Novello Davis (1893-1951) and dearly wanted the award. No wonder she stormed furiously out of the ceremony. An away defeat for the band then, Tossers 1 Cardiff 0.

So it was yet another snub for Catatonia. It was difficult not to view the media and the music industry aficionados as using Cerys for their own ends and repaying her by slapping her and the band in public whenever the opportunity arose.

Prior to the Margam Park concert, Aled explained one of the reasons behind choosing that particular venue. "Should be good. There's a lot of deer at Margam Park, so there's bound to be a bit of deer shit around. The show's about us doing our bit for Welsh culture. We're raising the people up from sheep shit to the more elevated realm of deer shit."

Cerys likened the Port Talbot Margam Park concert to a scene from the 80s film *Bladerunner*. "Port Talbot's got one of the most beautiful sights at night because it's got a huge oil refinery. It looks futuristic with lots of lights and tall buildings and flames. We're playing opposite. It's got a kind of natural amphitheatre kind of thing. There'll also be a fairground and fireworks."

May 29th was the date, Margam Park, Port Talbot was the venue. It was at the time the largest open-air pop festival held in Wales, although attendance-wise, it was subsequently beaten by the Stereophonics gig at Morfa. The setting was idyllic, the sideshows provided something for everyone. I have never seen as many Welsh flags all being waved or worn with pride.

Support acts for Catatonia were Richard Parfitt (ex-60ft Dolls), Big Leaves, Shack, Bjorn Again and special guest Ian Brown. As good and varied a bill as befitted the venue.

But it seemed as though the gig might be jinxed. An hour and a half before the public were admitted, the heavens opened. The rain was heavy and incessant. For a long time it looked as though it was here to stay, but by mid-afternoon it relented.

It was all my fault. I went, therefore it rained.

Clad in T-shirt, denim jeans and a non-waterproof Welsh flag, I was still damp and cold when I got home at 1.30 on Sunday morning. The problem was that the rain coincided with the arrival of the crowds, and therefore it became a sea of mud.

At some outdoor gigs, the front area is cordoned off and the first people in get wristbands, thus limiting the problems of congestion. This didn't happen at Margam. As Catatonia were preparing to take the stage at about 8.45pm, there was a surge which was to continue for about twenty minutes. The people at the front, including many families and groups of ladies and youngsters had stood there for seven hours in the rain supporting all the other bands. They were jostled and pushed to the floor by the horde of drunken zombies fresh from the beer tent. It was difficult to keep one's footing and the Security Staff could not get into the crowd to help. So it was left to us, the fans, to help those in distress over the barriers to the waiting Security Officers. It could so easily have been another Hillsborough disaster.

Cerys made an appeal for the crowd to move back but it was beyond her control. The request was cut from the TV coverage which featured some intruiging editing. First it was dusk when Catatonia took the stage yet some of the crowd shots appeared as if in daylight. Second, it did not show any of the crowd mayhem.

I don't condone violence, but I got some satisfaction from punching the wanker who thought it great fun to knock a lady and her two very small young children to the floor and then try to tread them into the ground to get to the front boasting, "That's what you get at pop concerts." He discovered that if you live by those rules, you can get more than you bargained for.

Earlier in the afternoon, Richard Parfitt succeeded in coaxing the rain to stop and played a short but tidy set. Big Leaves, Shack and Bjorn Again made excellent, though varied contributions. Ian Brown was very disappointing. He seemed to lose the plot as soon as he came on stage. His band made noble efforts to rescue the act, but Ian seemed to be more interested in slagging off the Welsh people in the crowd. With odds of 34,000 to 1 against, he was never going to win.

And then, the reason why the vast majority of people were there. The entrance of Catatonia. As they took the stage, Cerys shed her shocking pink, fake fur coat, revealing a glamorous, figure-hugging, silver sequined designer dress and matching gloves.

"When I was a little girl," she informed the crowd, "I dreamt I'd come back and haunt this place. It's nice to do it before I've died."

There seemed to be a few technical problems early on. Cerys faltered on "Game On" and she initially seemed uneasy with "Karaoke Queen" until part way through when she let it go full throttle.

Very, very occasionally, you see something that stays in your memory for a very long time. That night provided me with one such moment.

The Pontarddulais Male Voice Choir (who had also featured in the film *Twin Town*) sang a haunting, unaccompanied introduction to "Mulder and Scully". There was a slight pause. Aled drummed in, the guitars ripped the evening air apart and Cerys cruised in from backstage. She was like a Spanish galleon in full rigging cutting through the sparkling ocean, bringing home the spoils of battle. She smiled in sheer delight as she neared the front of the stage, to be met by a wall of sound as the crowd sang as one, "I'd rather be liberated". It happened in seconds, but that moment will last my lifetime.

"Road Rage" and "International Velvet" brought the best out of both band and crowd. Cerys' choice of dress limited some of her movements but she still managed to shimmy and slither across the front of the stage, milking every moment of adulation from the crowd. All the hard work that the band had put in was rewarded. Tears of joy and relief replaced the tears of despair she had shed when the rains set in.

During "International Velvet" Cerys confessed, "I was still crying! I was probably thinking about the great arguments we'd had beforehand regarding the choir and that."

"I just thought how cool the choir looked," added Owen.

Select magazine commented; "Maybe it's the way the screens, the lights and the crowd allow Catatonia to look – for the first time in their history

– genuinely heroic. Perhaps it's the fact that you'd be hard pushed to find a group who've played a gig this big after mid-career chapters involving such crushing frustration as theirs."

Nearly everybody there was sodden and covered in mud. Some had been sliding in it, others simply fell down or were brushed against by slime covered punters. After I got off my coach and started the walk home through Cardiff City centre, myself and others like me contrasted with the late night revelers in their designer leisure wear.

I had set off in all black, now I was 75% brown. Aled's words came back to me... I hoped to God that it was not deer shit that I was sporting.

The gig was televised in an edited version on BBC2 on Bank Holiday Monday. It was then that I noticed that when the camera focussed on Mark playing keyboards there were different coloured and shaped symbols on the keys. I later asked him what this meant. He truthfully replied that it was because he couldn't play the keyboards and the symbols were to guide him. In an industry where honesty is in short supply but egos are a-plenty, it was a refreshing admission.

Planning the *Home Internationals* had involved a lot of time and effort from the group and they wanted the concerts to be special. They certainly achieved their objective. The year had seen Catatonia storm the UK festival circuit and Cerys and the boys just wanted time out to sit on that success at home, rather than charge the circuit again and possibly not do as well. Thus, their decision to only play the Reading festival. It was a fine balance, because the fans would have loved to have seen more of them in the UK.

Cerys remembers something from the early days which supported their decision. "When we first started out as a band, I was really keen on doing a lot of gigs and showing off, and Mark used to say, 'No, just calm down and take it easy. Keep it special'. Otherwise if you're a band in the locality and they're playing every week, even their friends are fed up with listening. It becomes a habit."

In June of that year, London's National Portrait Gallery hosted a photographic exhibition entitled *Icons of Pop* (subtitled *from Cliff to Cerys*). The exhibition celebrated the top 50 performers of the last four decades. Cerys Matthews was included, having been photographed by Klanger and Boink in a pastiche of Jack Kerouac – moody, smoking a cigarette, dressed all in black and wearing a bell-boy's hat. The exhibition ran until September 6th.

The faces of the whole band were given further exposure to promote a campaign for 1999 being the "national year of reading". They were plastered on the sides of buses and could be seen cruising the streets of Cardiff, Swansea, Newport, Llanelli, Bangor, Llandudno and Rhyl. Life for the group then took a hectic turn.

Groningen in Holland was the setting for one of the concerts on the Rolling Stones European tour and Catatonia provided the support, bravely battling against foul and dangerous weather conditions. There was a huge electrical storm that played havoc with the site equipment. Lightning struck the 300ft production tower and mayhem was the watchword. Cerys remained undaunted. "During sound check we were going, 'Don't worry! We're safe!'" as the storm flashes lit up the stage and sky.

When they took to the stage it became worse. "It was that bad," she continued, "they were going, 'Get offstage! It's dangerous!' But we said no. And my dress went completely see-through. Owen was in more danger than me. I made sure I wore wellies."

The Rolling Stones were not aloof and were courteous to their guests. Owen and Cerys recalled, "They were actually brilliant." In fact Cerys added, "I think they drank the most, definitely. We were like little pussies compared to them."

Even so, she was a forced to admit, "We stayed in Amsterdam that night, but I don't remember much about Amsterdam."

Meanwhile, the lady herself was lapping up the fruits of success with invitations coming from all quarters. In mid-June, Donatella Versace held a Bond Street fashion ball, and she was one of the celebrities invited to attend.

Cardiff designer Kristin Ede has three distinguished Welsh clients. Ffion Hague, Catherine Zeta Jones and Cerys Matthews. Kristin grew up with Cerys and even helped her to develop her Welsh-with-attitude image.

"I've known Cerys since I was a teenager," recounts Kristin, "and I've seen her blossom from an arm-wrestling busker to a stylish woman. We've kept in touch and I've designed for her. I design clothes specifically for Welsh women, who tend to be a lot curvier than English women. I love the bright clubby clothes that Cerys wears."

Cardiff model, Sara Williams, is also a big fan of Cerys' individual look, which she says is copied by thousands of teenagers and proves the point that the secret of looking good has nothing to do with the size of your wallet.

No doubt armed with new clothes and accessories, Cerys joined up with the band to play two German concerts on June 26th and 27th. The South-side Festival was held at a huge old airport on the outskirts of Munich.

This was a newly launched event with a 25,000 capacity and was a sister-event to the Hurricane Festival held at Scheessel, which has a 50,000 capacity on two stages at a countryside speedway track. Germany seems to have a strange mixture of venues. These two venues I find as appealing as Bernard Manning's underpants, but then you have the beauty of Loreley which simply takes your breath away.

It was then the turn of Catatonia's management and record company to take centre stage in an embarrassing tug of war over what should be the next release from *Equally Cursed and Blessed*. "Karaoke Queen" was announced as due for release on June 21st (although a leading music journal had already stated it would be "Londinium"). While it was at production planning stage there was a change of plan and "Londinium" was selected and scheduled for release on July 12th.

Cerys explained; "We chose 'Karaoke Queen' originally but were advised it might not get as much radio play. I don't care which song it is, 'Karaoke Queen' or 'Londinium', as I have tremendous pride in all our three-minute compositions." She was to later take a more defiant stance over "Karaoke Queen", a song that she had written herself, but the damage had been done.

While all this confusion was raging, Cardiff's Millennium Stadium opened for business on June 26th, with Wales playing and beating the then World rugby champions South Africa by 29– 9. Prior to the game a Welsh Rugby Union Official promised everyone, "You won't be disappointed – it's sexy. The stadium is looking absolutely brilliant. It's a state of the art arena and it makes just as much a statement about Cool Cymru as Catatonia. And if you're not as stirred by the sight of the stadium as you are by Cerys Matthews, there's something missing."

Catatonia then flew to Europe to support REM for dates at Hanover on June 29th and Berlin on the 30th. During their gig at Wuhlheide in Berlin, REM suffered a stage invasion when Cerys got up to her old tricks and rushed on to give bassist Mike Mills a kiss. A spokeswoman for Catatonia said, "Matthews' behaviour was probably fuelled by a bottle of wine," and had left the more reserved Mills "rather shocked". "She just ran on, grabbed him and snogged him in the middle of a song. He looked rather taken aback. Despite this, the bands had got on really well."

Cerys admitted that the incident didn't go down particularly well with REM's Michael Stipe.

This was probably only the start of Mike Mills' problems as following the set he and Cerys indulged in an absinthe drinking session. "A drink to have among friends," she said, "It's just crazy. It puts you on a parallel universe, it's like, completely crazy."

Three days later, the group were back in England to contribute a mini-set along with a Who's Who of pop acts generally more at home miming. Hyde Park's *Party In The Park* on July 3rd featured Catatonia as surprise special guests. It was obviously a surprise to Steve Penk of Capital Radio, who introduced the band as Cerys Hughes and Catatonia.

They sang "Dead From The Waist Down" and "Londinium" and as usual, stole the show. It would have been nice if they had sung "Storm The Palace" for the benefit of Mr Windsor Jnr who was in the crowd.

Whether or not it was Cerys' way of showing that she did not dislike London, her top was conspicuously festooned with London souvenir badges. The show was recorded and televised at a later date featuring interviews with the stars before and after their appearances. The interviewer snatched a few words with Cerys on her way to the dressing room. She promptly raised her skirt to show the world a pair of mauve knickers, hardly broke stride and never stopped talking. This was the prelude to several gigs where Cerys seemed intent on showing us the contents of her underwear drawer.

Confusion still reigned over the band's next single and in a Radio 1 interview on July 5th Catatonia explained that they had had to change their minds about which song should be released. The band had wanted "Karaoke Queen" but radio programmers around the country were keener on "Londinium". This clearly ruffled Cerys' feathers and she claimed that while she was in the middle of recording she had received a call from someone in radio inviting her to promote a single she did not like.

More bad news was in store for the band when Warners dropped Catatonia from their label in America for the second time. Warners thought that the band were too pop and not alternative enough, therefore they could not promote *Equally Cursed and Blessed*. Almost immediately however, another label in the USA was making favourable noises, but at the time, Cerys, being forever superstitious, declined to name the company concerned. It later emerged to be Atlantic who subsequently signed up Catatonia.

Further evidence of increasing stress and strain was revealed on July 8th when the *Daily Telegraph* featured an interview with Cerys. Many references were made about her feeling tired and harassed.

"When she is told she is required in the make-up room, she becomes irritated. 'I don't like people fussing. It's what I hate the most. I hate it. Fuss,

fuss, fuss! There's always somebody who knows exactly what I'm gonna be doing, where I'm going, who I'm gonna speak to – and I don't. It's horrible. I've been going along merrily like a hamster in a wheel. Now I want to get off.'"

Twenty-six years earlier a little girl had thrown a tantrum in Cardiff Market because she felt sorry for the hamsters stuck in their cages. Despite her tears no one let them out. That little girl had grown up and was now looking out of the cage, hoping for a little respite, a chance to take stock and recharge her batteries. The enthusiasm and motivation were only there in patches now, and if no one listened to these cries for help they were in danger of being completely extinguished.

"Since the release of *International Velvet*," she continued, "it's been such a strange year – so busy. All of a sudden I just felt knackered. I haven't had a chance to get smashed and fiddle about on my piano at home for a long, long time, and I miss it. It was never fame I craved really. I never went to stage school, you know what I mean. There are some people who don't seem very fussy about how they get famous. I just wanted to be a great singer. Fame is the rod that breaks your back. You lose a lot of freedom."

When it was pointed out to her that she had previously said she wanted to be a "proper star" she said, "Look at me. I'm getting tired of it aren't I?"

This was the interview that caused those close to the band to start worrying. She had obviously been fraught during some of her public appearances and interviews in 1999, although it is to her credit that she still delivered the goods on stage. After almost eighteen months of continuous gigging at home and overseas, along with a mountainous schedule of promotional work, it was easy to see why. There was also a personal life to try and fit in. It has happened all too often before. The entertainment business, more than any other, kills the goose that lays the golden egg.

The warning lights were flashing. Good management is about getting the maximum return from your assets, but when your assets are human beings then you have to be very understanding and caring in order to keep them in good shape. True, the band were ambitious to cash in while the going was good and were prepared to work to that goal, but it was becoming obvious that the record company and the band seemed to have different views about the path to follow. I could not recall Blanco Y Negro having success on this scale before and perhaps they were unsure of how to deal with it. After seeing the band underachieve for so long in the past, it was hurting me to witness what was happening now that they were finally reaping some success.

WHEN FACED WITH MY DEMONS

If you look at the world today, there's a lot wrong with it, and, at the end of the day, I can put my hand on my heart and say I mean well.

Cerys Matthews

If it can go wrong, it will go wrong. The latter half of 1999 certainly played its part in proving this as far as Catatonia were concerned. It was a time of confusion, rumour and speculation. To make matters worse, the press arrived at phase three of their coverage of all things Catatonia. The warmth and loyalty of the Catatonia fan-base remained, but even they were becoming confused about what was going on behind the scenes.

But it was not to be all doom and gloom. They were still in huge demand for festivals and events. Forever the troopers, the band went back into Western Europe and Scandinavia. MIDTIFYNS was a five-day festival held on a small island off the coast of Jutland between July 7th and 11th, and featured an appearance from Catatonia along with a host of other bands including Massive Attack.

Cerys remembered seeing a Finnish lesbian singer and naked people running around, but this was not the strangest sight to greet her eyes, as ships were apparently passing on dry land. "There were these massive ferries going past with most of the bulk above water because they weren't loaded. I didn't even know there was a river there! Then this fucking huge tanker goes past!"

In July, Cerys was voted "The Coolest Person in Pop" by the readers of *Melody Maker*. It was explained to her that the award was for the coolest person and not just lady. This really pleased her because she associates "cool" with not being obnoxious.

Also around this time there was an "ask and tell" session on "Adam's Catatonia Homepage" which involved members of the band. Questions came in from all over the world. Many topics were covered, but one European fan enquired when Catatonia would be undertaking a tour of Western Europe. Owen mentioned that a tour was scheduled for November. This information was to assume more significance later in the year.

As far as the present was concerned, despite all the shennanigans, their next single, "Londinium", was released on July 12th in CD, 7" vinyl, and cassette form. The B-sides were "Apathy Revolution" (CD only) and "Intercontinental Sigh".

It reached a highest chart position of number 20. The accompanying video, again directed by Patricia Murphy, symbolises life in London as a fishbowl. Catatonia, are seen inside the bowl, singing and playing underwater as ornamental fish float by. Pearly Kings and Queens try to grab the band members, who finally escape through a sewer and steal a London cab.

With a long, dark-haired Cerys at the wheel, they return to Wales, portrayed as a paradise of green fields, blue skies, a rainbow and a blue sea. Mermaids wave as Cerys dives in and plunges towards the sea bed, savouring the natural waves, after the stale water of the fishbowl. The sun goes down. Cerys was to describe the video as "Amphibious, underwater, overexpensive, over-sinister and over my dead body."

The fuss that surrounded the release of this record was unbelievable. The music press jokingly, but pointedly, printed photos of Cerys and her friends entering bars in London. The media interviewed various inhabitants of the city, including a spokesman for the Soho branch of Yo Sushi, who said, "I haven't heard the song, but if it criticises Sushi bars then obviously we don't agree with it. London's a cosmopolitan city and we contribute to that." Cerys loves most things Japanese, especially the food, and is well known for eating in Sushi bars, especially Yo Sushi, where she has regularly been for meals with her friends.

The band had been singing the song live at gigs for eight months and seemingly there was no problem. I know a lot of Londoners who thought the song was brilliant and reflected their opinions. Their feelings were about those people who use London purely to make money. Significantly it was this type of person who objected. No wonder Welsh rugby fans sing, "You can stick your fucking chariots up your arse."

Cerys assured fans that she liked London despite the thrust of the lyrics. For all those who claimed to be offended by the song, it was so nice to see "Cardiff suck the F.A.Cup out of you," whilst Wembley Stadium undergoes repairs.

She then admitted that she was anxious to return to Wales, having been away for three weeks, because her friend Sioned, who she shares a house with, had given birth to a 7lb 8oz baby son.

"I've gotta get used to having a baby in the house," she said, "I'm very excited, 'cos I've never really lived with a baby before, apart from a couple of ex-boyfriends!"

It was also revealed that the band were planning to retreat to Wales to write new material, probably not for release until the end of 2000.

Meanwhile in Wales, artists such as the Manic Street Preachers, Catatonia, Gorky's Zygotic Mynci, Super Furry Animals and Spiritualized had all written music for an album of poetry by Patrick Jones, brother of the Manic's Nicky Wire. The album entitled *Commemoration and Amnesia* was released on July 19th.

Prior to the release of the album, Patrick Jones was asked if he thought the Welsh Assembly was a good idea. He replied, "Even parties like Plaid Cymru skirt around the real issues. I know bands like the Manics and Catatonia are rich now, but at least they sing about the real issues, the deprivation and the pain."

The current issue that was causing Catatonia pain was the new single. The debate over "Londinium" continued. On Channel 4's *Big Breakfast* Cerys said she would have rather released another track off *Equally Cursed and Blessed* because a lot of people thought it a negative song, but the record company executives and their management had insisted on "Londinium". She further complained that the video had cost a lot more to make than the album, thus providing further indication of the growing differences between band, management and record company.

This was certainly not the year to mess about with Cerys. She was still likely to be tetchy in interviews and in her public profile. The Cerys of 1999 was very different to the Cerys of 1998. She had shown that she could go from being incredibly high in spirits to being absolutely drained within a very short period of time. The writing was on the wall, but nobody seemed to be reading it. Maybe because I had been on similar ground myself, or perhaps I had a sixth sense where Catatonia were concerned, but the problem was obvious to me. So why not to the people who she was working for? The band's management refused to comment on her outburst on television, other than to say, "We love all the album".

Top Of The Pops on July 22nd featured Catatonia singing "Londinium" which had just charted at number 20. Cerys wore a tiara, fake diamond necklace and a T-shirt with a heart containing the letters VD – a reference to Victoria Adams and David Beckham's coat of arms and lavish wedding. A TV insider said, "Cerys was so appalled by the wedding, she just wanted to tell viewers about it. It's just harmless fun."

With all the fuss over the record, a journey to the Southern hemisphere must have been most welcome. Australia had taken Catatonia to their hearts and the band scheduled a short stopover tour to play the Hi Fi Bar Melbourne and the Metro in Sydney, between July 24th and 28th en-route to the Fuji Festival in Japan.

When the tour was announced, it was suggested that the prospect of Tokyo, with its neon lights and vibrant nightlife would be a very alluring prospect, but Cerys insisted she fancied gardening. "I can check out some blossom and some Japanese gardens. I just love their minimalist approach. It's really gorgeous when you can be driven out to somewhere in the countryside. So I really wanna do that in Japan."

Despite arriving at 4am, the band was greeted by cheering fans at Melbourne airport. At the gig the band played a mixture of songs from the last two albums before an enthusiastic, Welsh flag flying, antipodean audience of about 1,500. Merthyr meets Melbourne. The band played well, augmented by Cerys swaying provocatively in her slinky white dress. You could tell it wasn't the UK because at the end of the show the stage was covered in flowers thrown by fans rather than the now customary female sanitary products.

Everett True, a reporter who had covered Catatonia on many previous occasions was there for *Melody Maker*. After the first Melbourne gig, Cerys accosted him and his partner and they went to a karaoke bar, where Cerys still had the energy to sing solo and duet versions of "Some Enchanted Evening", "Blackbird", "Do You Want To Know A Secret", "I Should Be So Lucky", "To Sir With Love" and "Danny Boy".

The following evening, the band and reporter visited a local bar. Cerys was surrounded by Aussie Rules footballers, while Mark checked his watch and wondered what his mates back home were doing ("drinking in the pub, I reckon"). In a world of chaos, it is refreshing that some things stay the same.

It was then on to Sydney where the band played two gigs to similar sized audiences. A spokesperson for Catatonia confirmed, "The band really enjoyed them, because it had been a long time since they had played shows that intimate."

On the earlier trip, spare time had been at a premium, "but this time we managed a day off," explained Cerys, "and went to a National Park to see the marsupials. The boys saw the Koala Bears, I never did, but I saw some kangaroos. This kangaroo had a hard on, and this little American kid was next to me going, 'Look, Daddy! There's a baby kangaroo there!'

"I'm going, 'It's a penis!'"

Leaving the upstanding marsupial to its own devices, Catatonia jetted off to Japan to play at the Mount Fuji Rock Festival alongside the Happy Mondays, Fun Lovin' Criminals, Blur, The Chemical Brothers, Ocean Colour Scene and Hole.

The band played early in the day with Cerys sporting a towel she had borrowed from their hotel. It was also the first time that the band had played in front of an audience sporting parasols.

After completing their set, they had time to walk around the site and watch the other bands, with Ocean Colour Scene being one that particularly took their interest. To relax in the heat, Cerys took off her shoes and sat in a nearby stream. She obviously thought Steven Craddock from OCS needed cooling down so she promptly pushed him in.

Catatonia's record company in Japan then invited Cerys for a night out in Tokyo, where appropriately, she found herself singing in a karaoke bar with some very drunk businessmen until the early hours. That was the only night the band had off.

While Catatonia were in Japan, they were interviewed for *Fine* (a Japanese magazine) by Kiyomi Multi Color (that is her stage name – she is the singer with a Japanese pop band, Astro-B). During the very relaxed interview, Cerys enjoyed sampling some sake. In addition to talking about the festival, she mentioned she had plans to transform her house into the Japanese style and had bought, amongst other things, yukata (a kimono for the summer), and noren (a curtain with a bamboo stick). Owen somewhat obtusely added that "sticks were rare in Cardiff".

Afterwards, Kiyomi presented Cerys with a tenugui (Japanese towel) and some sake.

The band then flew home for a couple of weeks break.

Next on the agenda were two European festivals as the 1999 game plan seemed to be to reach as many of their fans as possible around the world.

August 21ˢᵗ saw them appear at the Bizarre Festival in Cologne, Germany. Cerys was in good form between the songs, displaying her unique and lovable disregard for political correctness. After concluding "She's a Millionaire" she addressed the crowd. "We were staying in our hotel in Cologne last night, watching the concert on MTV. Did you see Marilyn Manson? What a twat Marilyn Manson is. What a fucking twat! So this is for him anyway – 'Karaoke Queen'."

The following day, Aug 22ⁿᵈ, Catatonia played at the Vilar de Mouros Festival in Portugal. "It was in the middle of nowhere, on the side of a mountain," recalls Cerys, "and I remember looking at all the flowers. It was beautiful. But it started at ten at night, and went on all night long. I thought I played one of the worst gigs of my life."

This was soon compensated for when Catatonia appeared as special guests of Blur on the Main Stage at the Reading Festival '99. They played the Reading site on August 28ᵗʰ and the Leeds site on the 29ᵗʰ.

Reports alleged that Cerys was refusing to appear at Reading unless she was supplied with a bath full of champagne. This could have been a publicity stunt or a further demonstration that all was not well. Difficult to say as the source was the tabloids.

The boys were already on stage when Cerys entered slowly and seductively, stage left, wearing a totally revealing gold fishnet gown, with a set of matching burgundy underwear. Cerys later told *Melody Maker*, "I was surprised at the reaction it got. It wasn't that bad. Nice pair of pants and bra." And this is from a lady who professes that she is into clashing underwear. It was that kind of outfit. It was that kind of performance.

Catatonia played an outstanding set. With the quality of material in their locker they just steamrollered their way to proving they were the best band there. Between songs, Cerys mentioned she had been "chicken, for letting Radio 1 chose their last single."

The band played Leeds the following day. Cerys considered that they gave a far better display there. I gave Leeds a miss. Whilst recovering from that musical and visual feast, fans in Britain were delighted with the announcement on August 31ˢᵗ of a six-venue UK arena tour starting at Glasgow SECC on December 5ᵗʰ and concluding at Cardiff International Arena on December 13ᵗʰ. Home-based fans had felt a little starved of appearances, as most of Catatonia's live gigs this year had been overseas. However, for me, fate was moving in mysterious ways.

Research for this book had been a labour of love, and on September 7ᵗʰ I asked for some information via one of the unofficial Catatonia websites.

I also mentioned my work with bands in Wales. One of Catatonia's genuine keenest fans replied, asking me if I only worked with Welsh groups, because two of her friends were in a band and were currently on holiday in the UK and at the same time were seeking to promote themselves.

Apparently, Catatonia, were a big influence on this band and I readily agreed to meet them. They came to Cardiff from London to see me on the 9th and I tried to show them places of interest, particularly those associated with Catatonia folklore. They were Kiyomi and Riuygi from Japanese band Astro-B, who had interviewed Catatonia in Tokyo only one month earlier, along with the lady who contacted me, Margot Saint. Proof of her love for Catatonia was demonstrated when she left South Wales to watch Catatonia play their gigs in Japan in November 1999. We retired to the City Arms (where else?) and discussed the ways in which I could try and help Astro-B.

Coincidentally, Astro-B had left a demo of their music with Rough Trade and had also given Tommy Scott from Space a copy at the Reading Festival. Was this meeting destiny? Has the wheel gone round full circle? I don't know how many times I have said, "With Catatonia, expect the unexpected."

Another piece of work outside the band saw Cerys record "Baby it's Cold Outside" with Tom Jones on his album of collaborations entitled *Reload*. The album was released at the end of September and the single scheduled for December 6th. She was in demand for other work and was asked to record a version of the 1966 classic "The More I See You" for the romantic comedy film *Fanny and Elvis*. Also "Thank Your Stars" for *Watership Down* and "We'll Gather Lilacs" along with "Bugeilio'r Gwenyth Gwyn" for a then untitled Sara Sugarman film in which Cerys was to have a brief acting cameo role. Cerys diary was bursting at the seams fitting in solo and group projects.

Appropriately, "International Velvet" performed by Catatonia was a key feature in the Opening Ceremony of Rugby Union's World Cup in Cardiff's Millennium stadium on October 2nd. I was in the ground in spirit, because I had, for the only time in my life, loaned my Welsh/Catatonia flag to someone I could trust. It had to be there. I couldn't be.

Before a capacity crowd in their home city, the band took to the centre of the pitch at 2 o'clock, welcomed by a deafening roar from the crowd. On stage, Cerys removed her black coat to reveal her beloved red, Welsh rugby shirt and spangly trousers. The cheers round the stadium made grown men cry. The layer of glitter around her eyes emphasised the immense pride flowing from her, as both the band and crowd unified in a glorious pageant of patriotism and internationalism. 'International Velvet', the anthem that was not intended as such, finally proved Mark wrong. As Cerys' voice was drowned by the crowd, I was stood in the City Arms watching this on big screen TV with tears in my eyes, as a Roberts/Catatonia song got the response it deserved.

I was an Englishman crying with joy in a Welsh pub, surrounded by my Welsh friends and many strangers, and I didn't give a fuck. A song originally intended to foster internationalism had been taken to a nation's heart, but when sung in the national stadium it moved a worldwide audience. As a bonus, the album *International Velvet* soared back up the album charts for two weeks.

Whilst nations had united in sport for the World Cup, the situation in Kosovo had demonstrated once again, man's inhumanity to man. On October 9th the NetAid concert was organised at three venues and was webcast live, in an attempt to raise funds for the refugee crisis. Catatonia played at Wembley Stadium in front of over 70,000 fans. "This is the biggest pub we've ever done," Cerys stated with a glazed smile, clad in a sexy fishnet top with a strategically placed heart motif.

Melody Maker summed their performance up succinctly. "Coming from a band with a self-confessed support band mentality, the spiraling glory of 'Do You Believe In Me?' doesn't half sound like the biggest band in the world slumming it at the arse end of the bill. Sublime."

Afterwards the artists were asked, "What difference can a charity event like NetAid make?" Cerys responded, "It will make fuck all difference. But the truth is, we've got to try. We got involved because Harvey Goldsmith asked us and we were too young to do Live Aid. On July 13th, 1985 the wine had been flowing all afternoon but I heard it was really good from my older sister. This is a worldwide thing, that's why I got involved." It was noticeable that Cerys was starting to use "I" in interviews quite regularly, as opposed to "we".

The band's supporters took heart from the performance but they were hit by a bombshell on October 10th when it was announced that the December arena tour had been cancelled.

An official statement was issued.

Dear all,

After much soul searching and thought we have unfortunately decided to cancel our forthcoming UK tour. We don't want to use the usual excuses – production problems, visa problems etc, etc.

The simple truth is that after 22 months of whirlwind success we need a break and as a band haven't been able to put together a new show we'd be proud of. By charging ahead with the tour we feel we wouldn't be doing justice to ourselves, or to our magnificent fans who have supported us through thick and thin.

We know many people will be disappointed – for this we apologise, but feel in our hearts that this is the best course of action for all of us.

We will be back better and stronger next year.

Thank you for everyone's support.

Diolch am y cefnogaeth a phopeth arall efo cariad mawr.

Aled, Cerys, Mark, Owen and Paul.

The initial reaction amongst the fans was predictable. The statement was viewed with the same suspicion as when a football club chairman says he has every confidence in his manager. It is a Catch-22 situation. You give an official explanation and nobody wants to believe it. Rumours immediately started to fly around.

- One of the band was seriously ill.
- The band was splitting up.
- Cerys was going solo.
- Cerys would be too busy plugging "Baby It's Cold Outside" with Tom Jones to bother with Catatonia.
- Cerys was having treatment for alcohol abuse.
- Ticket sales had been so low that the management had pulled the plug on the tour.
- One of the band was pregnant (I do not know which one they meant).

There were many more ludicrous ideas as to why the tour was cancelled. In fact some were totally unbelievable and not repeatable. A lot of fans lost money, myself included, because we forfeited part of the booking fee. Unfortunately, it goes with the territory.

What really did anger fans in the UK was the announcement made the following day by their management that Catatonia were undertaking a ten-gig European tour starting at Copenhagen Vega on November 16th and finishing at Malmo KB on November 28th. In fairness it was the tour that Owen had referred to in July on the internet, and had obviously been planned long ago, but the timing could not have been worse. If the band were too tired to play the UK arena tour, then why tour Europe and Japan?

Was there any significance in cancelling the arena gigs the day after the NetAid concert?

Management explained the reason for cancelling the UK tour via a spokeswoman.

"The band have a new single "Karaoke Queen" coming out at the beginning of November and around that they will be up for doing *Top of The Pops*, *TFI* and whatever. They have a job to do and they will promote it. They're not suddenly going to be in the wilderness.

"Somebody had to say, 'We're already burnt out. Now we've got this coming up, that coming up and with the single release and everything that that involves, are we realistically going to be in any frame of mind, come December, to do a tour and to do it justice?'

"They really have been non-stop for 22 months. They had the dates with the Manics at the end of last year. Straight from that they recorded an album and two-and-a-half months later the album was out, so the touring starts all over again. They have never really taken that break, had a deep breath which maybe they should have done.

"Up until that time, the band had never really had the pressures of when the rest of the world kicks in and when all the territories want time from you. They were suddenly at the point when Europe was saying, 'Come out here,' and Japan was saying, 'We're releasing singles, come out here.' They've been to Australia and New Zealand twice.

"They've gone straight from one record to another record, they've been getting pulled this way and that, and they should maybe have had a bit more rest really."

The statement contained a number of anomolies. Firstly, according to the music press and interviews given by the band, the album was recorded and mixed before the Manics tour; it was just a little fine tuning which took place afterwards.

Secondly, the responsibility for the group not having had a break from working in 22 months lay with the management and record company. There did not seem to be any coherent strategy. For instance, for a group to visit Japan, Australia and New Zealand twice in under ten months for mini-tours is ridiculous. Surely, one visit with more gigs would have been wiser and less stressful on the group.

Lastly, the management had all this information to hand before they announced the UK tour, so why was such a tour even contemplated? Anybody would have been shattered with the workload the band had undertaken. A seemingly endless programme of concerts, recording and promotional work. It's amazing that they had not collapsed on stage.

However, the only information that came my way was from "a pal" who has contacts at the ticket offices. He informed me that bookings had not really taken off and that sales for the Cardiff International Arena in particular had been disappointing. The gigs were in the run up to Millennium Eve and a lot of people were saving money for that particular night.

Despite the original hassle and uncertainty surrounding "Karaoke Queen", it was chosen to be the next single release. CD1 had "Karaoke Queen (remix)", "Don't Wanna Talk About It" and "All Girls Are Fly (Da – De remix)". CD2 was a 3" Japanese style mini-disc featuring "Karaoke Queen (remix edit)", "Karaoke Queen (remix edit) Karaoke" and "Dead From The Waist Down – Karaoke." The cassette and 7" vinyl contained "Karaoke Queen (remix)" and "Don't Wanna Talk About It".

Patricia Murphy directed the video. Based around a hospital ward that appeared to be hosting a talent show, Cerys was a contestant and the band were the judges. Catatonia's concern about the lack of backing that farmers were getting from the government in the wake of the BSE crisis was highlighted in the video. At the beginning of the contest a calf called "Cattletonia" appears wearing a £2 price tag (its then price) and it finishes up at the end of the contest with a tag of £80 (its former price).

Cerys stated, "People probably think I'm bonkers having a calf in a pop video, but the politicians don't seem to be making any effort to help, so I thought I would."

The video also caused some controversy because it included transvestite dancers. MTV objected to certain parts of it. Because of this, and because there had to be the right remix (by Julian Mendlesohn), the release date was put back to November 1st. The record charted very disappointingly at 36.

Promoting the single on *TFI Friday* on October 29th the transvestite dancers appeared in the set and Cerys was noticeably unsteady on her feet, but the following day on BBC's children's programme *Live and Kicking* the dancers were replaced by actual ladies. It was stated on *Live and Kicking* that Cerys was having problems with her throat and voice.

The distribution of the record was farcical. Fans throughout the UK complained that their local record stores did not have a single copy. Cardiff was no exception. I went to a high street record shop there to buy all formats of the record only to be told by an assistant that Catatonia could not have released the record because they hadn't received a copy.

I went to Spillers (a small, independent record shop in Cardiff which was established in 1894 and claims to be the oldest record shop in the world) and bought all the formats.

It is very difficult for a record to chart if people cannot buy the record. There cannot be many other instances where a record from a major group has not been available in all high street record shops during the week of its release.

Once again, with a single to promote in the UK the band was sent to play gigs out of the country. Japan was next on the itinerary and Catatonia planned to play four gigs, starting at the Club Quatro in Osaka on November 4th and concluding at its sister club in Tokyo on November 8th. However, due to Cerys suffering from throat problems, a gig in Nagoya was cancelled.

I bumped into Mark's girlfriend in Cardiff and she asked if I knew what the mid-week position of "Karaoke Queen" was because she was telephoning Mark later. It was number 39 at that stage.

Meanwhile in the Land of the Rising Sun, Margot Saint was doing a valiant job teaching Kiyomi all the words (English and Welsh) of "International Velvet" which they, and the other members of the travelling Welsh contingent and their Australian friends, sang before the start of one of the Tokyo gigs.

Shortly after the band's return to the UK, the storm clouds started to gather. *Melody Maker* had a feature called Psychobabble, in which a star was asked a series of questions, some of which were tongue in cheek, ludicrous or weird. They were meant to be taken in fun. In the December 1st issue it was Cerys Matthews' turn to be quizzed. One question was to open up a can of worms. The worms in question worked for the tabloids.

Question: If you were to discover that your closest friend was a heroin dealer, what would you do?

Cerys: "I'd get some stuff off them cheaply. I think there's worse things in the world."

So Cerys gave a throwaway answer – the sort that the question deserved, and in fairness probably expected. This was not a serious article attempting to analyse the country's drugs problem. On checking back copies, I found that far worse answers had been given in Psychobabble.

A previous issue of the magazine had a lengthy feature that dealt with stars describing their drug usage. But the gutter press chose not to pick up on those.

The next day, Thursday December 2nd, all hell broke loose. *The Welsh Mirror* showed Cerys on the front page with the headline, "Outrage at Cerys heroin boast" – "Star says she'd buy deadly drug." The answer was twisted as far as possible to portray Cerys in the wrong light. In the accompanying article, anti-drugs campaigners alleged she had no brain. She was accused of sending the wrong messages to youngsters and that she should get off her millionaire backside and see the damage that drugs cause. Because she is a star, kids follow her example. *The South Wales Echo* followed suit and readers sent letters advocating banning Catatonia from playing in the area, boycotting their records and taking away Cerys' Welsh nationality.

I wrote to the *Echo* to put the article in perspective so that the readers could make their own minds up when presented with the true facts of the matter. They never published mine or any other letter on this issue. But the gist was:

Firstly, Cerys gave a hypothetical answer to a hypothetical question. If the answer was in bad taste then surely the question was. Secondly, the readership of the original article were used to this type of situation anyway and were probably not influenced one way or the other. It is the weakest excuse in the world to say that people follow what celebrities do, and as long as they trot that cliché out then the problem will never be solved.

Cerys smokes and drinks, which according to doctors are also very bad for your health. Both are habit forming and can be terminal, but the press didn't choose to criticise her for that. Basically, because these potentially addictive and killer drugs are socially acceptable.

The Welsh Mirror was so upset and concerned that the message was reaching youngsters and its thrust was that we must protect them and all other youngsters from reading such statements.

Their solution to ensure kids were not exposed to such statements was one of astounding simplicity. Splash it over the front page thereby spreading the gospel that they considered was irresponsible to the very people they alleged were vulnerable. All I can say is that in the years that I have followed the band, I have never heard Cerys recommend to other people that they should take drugs.

Whilst researching this book, I was informed that senior editorial staff were absent from the offices of the *Welsh Mirror* when this story ran, and that a more experienced eye would have not have treated it in the same way. Unfortunately, the damage had been done.

On BBC TV's *Question Time* the matter was brought up again. Welsh Secretary Paul Murphy MP, Conservative MP Nigel Evans, and Plaid Cymru's Helen Mary Jones, collectively stated that as a role model she should be more careful and should have a closer look at the effects of drugs on people. They considered it a flippant remark and that it could encourage kids to take drugs.

I seriously began to wonder if this panel were on something themselves. Had someone infiltrated the hospitality suite?

Cerys was dismayed at the outcome. "I am shocked that the *Welsh Mirror* has taken a flippant remark by me out of context and has reported it as me condoning the use of heroin. Nothing is further than the truth. I support the work done by drug rehabilitation charities and nothing I say is intended to undermine them."

Cerys' spokeswoman told *Melody Maker* that the remarks had been "completely blown out of all proportion", making the lead item on BBC news in Wales. "On the news they were saying Cerys did not mind heroin pushers, which totally misconstrued the whole thing." The spokeswoman said of Cerys, "I think she was quite upset."

Many people, some fans included, thought Cerys really should be getting wise to some of the pitfalls of being interviewed by now, but then if she did not shoot from the hip she would not be the Cerys that people admire so much.

The internet was hot with people from around the world seeking clarification, others assuring that support would be there from the fanbase if needed. I received over 30 emails from outside the UK alone, some from friends and some from people who must have picked up my address via websites. They were all requesting details because their press had picked up on the story. I gave them the facts from both sides, without venturing any opinion of my own.

Everyone replied and sympathised with Cerys for the treatment she had suffered at the hands of the media and pledged their support. There were even teams of fans in Cardiff who were prepared to stand next to every newspaper vendor and hand out flyers to anyone who bought the *South Wales Echo* just to give them the full story. Not to influence them – just to give them the facts so people could arrive at their own decision.

If you think I am over-reacting then please consider this example. Gary Holton had a modicum of success in the pop world in the seventies band the Heavy Metal Kids and later tried his hand at acting. He was in the successful ITV drama series *Auf Wiedersein Pet* and I met him when he was working on location on the second series. It was to be a very short friendship. He had a strong personality and like all of us he was not perfect. One of the tabloids then published stories about him at regular intervals exposing details about his private life. I do not know, or care, how true these stories were, but they hurt him deeply. Far deeper than he let on. Soon after he died of a drugs overdose.

His death was reported in the tabloids with touching concern. I have neither forgiven nor forgotten the treatment he received. It would appear that a hell of a lot of Catatonia fans feel the same way about the tabloid treatment of Cerys. Selling papers is one thing, but human life is far too precious.

The *Welsh Mirror* also featured an article about Tom Jones and Cerys which could have put thoughts of a romance between the two into readers minds. Were they trying to break this beautiful Welsh butterfly on the wheel, to paraphrase a famous sixties quote?

Cerys' duet with Tom Jones, "Baby It's Cold Outside", was released on December 6th. It received more promotional hype than any Catatonia record. They sang it on *Red Alert (Lottery Show), CD UK, Smash Hits Poll Winners Party, Pepsi Chart Show, TFI Friday* and *Top Of The Pops*. It was *Melody Maker's* Single of the Week.

Some of the shows featured interviews with the duo as well. The tabloids reported that Cerys refused to appear on *CDUK* unless she was given a bottle of champagne. I questioned the accuracy of this story and was assured that it was true because it had come from an insider at the TV company.

The record charted at number 18. The song itself is just a standard ballad. No more, no less. However, it provided Cerys with a vehicle to demonstrate that she can role-play in a song. She camped it up brilliantly. I am not the only one to notice that on some of the appearances Tom Jones was looking a little uncomfortable at the way Cerys totally stole the song and the limelight.

The Sun then hinted at Cerys' "friendship" with Tom Jones, whereas the *Mirror* told us a piece of history, disguised as news, namely that Tommy D and Cerys had split up. *Melody Maker*, so long a good friend of Catatonia, and unwitting instigator of the whole sorry drug affair, also put the boot in. They wondered how Cerys was too tired to play with Catatonia but was still fit enough to work with Tom Jones and reported that she may be going to Las Vegas to see him.

Cerys' spokeswoman explained. "No, she's not going to be singing with Tom Jones. All she was thinking of doing was going out on holiday to the USA, including a stop-off to go and see Tom Jones in Las Vegas. But she's not even going now."

Melody Maker did include Cerys as the pop star for August in their 2000 calendar. However, as the Millennium approached, Catatonia's diary did not seem overly full in terms of gigs.

Their main aim was to retire to Wales and commence work on a new album. This album could be a very critical one and the intention of the band was to give it their best shot which meant them making some surprising sacrifices, including declining top bookings at the main festivals in the year 2000. Insider information told me that they could have headlined at Glastonbury if they had been available.

1999 had seen a fair quota of gigs, mostly overseas. There had been a high quality number one album that in itself was a considerable achievement. But the sales of the singles from the album were hugely disappointing. It is easy to say that there were better songs on the album that could have been released, but that does not offer any solution. Certainly, the B-sides that accompanied the singles taken from *Equally Cursed and Blessed* were not as demanding of attention as their previous B-sides. There didn't seem to be that tightness, closeness or conviction in the songs that there had been in the past. Oh for a return of some joint Matthews/Roberts compositions to add to the repertoire.

Had Catatonia been led back to under-achieving?

Most importantly, could Cerys come to terms with whatever had been troubling her, and how would it affect the band?

Clearly the band was marking time when they should have been leading the way.

BLOW THE MILLENNIUM. BLOW

*The great bands of history prove themselves by how you chose to weave yourself
through time.*

Cerys Matthews

Herald in the new century. A time for putting things right and shaping
your destiny. Most people seemed to view the Millennial event as the
opportunity to be positive and creative. If you had been troubled in the
last century then now you could start again.

If only life were so simple.

Catatonia certainly seemed to have a lot to sort out. It was a time to
have a break, take stock and plan their future. In the words of "Tourist":
"*Conductor/ Tell the driver stop the bus/ I'm getting off/ I've had enough.*" Later
in the year, Cerys would admit that she had come perilously close to
making that decision.

As the Millennium dawned, *The Sun* and Channel 4 TV's *Void* teletext
both informed that, "Cerys Matthews is tipped to wed boyfriend Anthony
Glenn. They have been dating six months since she split from Catatonia
producer Tommy D."

On January 7th, I was in the company of a couple of band members, and
said, "It's typical, I just finish the first draft of the book and Cerys decides
to get married." Their response confirmed that she had got engaged and
that it was OK to include this in the book.

Twelve months earlier Cerys had been the sweetheart of the media and such news would have been manna from heaven for certain sections of the press. There would have been widespread coverage by the tabloids, pictures galore and the usual quota of rumours etc. But, now there was hardly anything reported.

Had she lost her magic touch?

Some suggested that it was a publicity stunt.

The year 2000 would see the band concentrate on working on their new album, but the challenging prospect of another attempt at the US market was in the offing. To this effect they performed two gigs in the USA in January 2000 to promote their pending new record releases Stateside. Atlantic Records spent time pushing the band and stressed in its publicity that their latest acquisition featured "a lovely young woman called Cerys Matthews". The band was typically referred to as indie-pop in the USA.

On January 24th they played the Bowery Ballroom in New York City. Whilst the band enjoyed both gigs on this trip, this one was special. Andrew Taber, writing for the influential *New York Times* was full of praise in his review of the gig.

Cerys looked stunning as usual, appearing in a black T-shirt, jeans and a soon-to-be discarded white jacket. Her current fashion preference meant that she wore black and white glamour eye make-up. With the perspiration generated by the energy of her performance, the make-up ran and she started to resemble one of the characters from "Dazed, Beautiful and Bruised". Typically, she captured the hearts of the audience as she swigged from her wine bottle. She came across as the typical USA female anti-heroine. Like Janis Joplin, but without the terminal angst. The atmosphere generated by the band was emotionally electric. For one night, at least, the pride of Cymru were the toast of this part of New York.

The day before the LA gig, the highly respected American music journal *Billboard* enthusiastically reviewed the pending release of "Road Rage" as a single and forecast good times for the band, again focussing on Cerys.

After the gig on the 27th, some of the band stayed on in the States. Cerys revealed later that she telephoned fiance Anthony Glenn from the USA on Valentines Day and broke off their engagement. However the relationship was to continue and the pair were together at the Brit Awards.

Cerys confirmed her disappointment at losing out at the Brits the previous year. She expressed her opinion that the Brits usually run a year behind the times and that she thought Catatonia might win something at the next one. The venue was Earls Court, on March 3rd 2000.

Catatonia had not been nominated for anything. I saw three members of the band in Cardiff that night, but Cerys had work to do, having been chosen to present the award for "Best Live Act". She took to the task, looking typically relaxed and in control and chatted with presenter Davina McCall before announcing the winners – Steps.

I also happened to notice that most of the nominations for "Best British Male Vocalist" were even older than me. I had seen these guys in black and white and it brought back memories. One of the nominees, who I shall not name, once bought me a pint of beer back in the late 1960s. It would then have cost 2 shillings. I never got an opportunity to buy him one back. If I get the chance, I will, but he can forget the Remy Martin at £65 a shot.

After the show Cerys headed off to a celebrity party organised by record company BMG at the Home House club. Also at this bash were the Stereophonics, Chris Evans, Tom Jones, Natalie Imbruglia and many others.

On the Monday, *The Sun* alleged that Cerys Matthews spent a long time chatting up Tom Jones. Working for *The Sun* he may not be aware that the pair originate from South Wales; work in the same industry; have recorded as a duo and have both admitted to being great friends and enjoying each other's company.

In keeping with the optimism surrounding the Millenium, the Welsh Music Foundation was created in January. One of the key roles of the WMF is to ensure that Wales develops a thriving music infrastructure by encouraging greater investment from the music industry and local businesses. The objective being to take future Welsh pop music to an international audience. Huw Williams and Natasha Hale, who had an involvement in the formative years of Catatonia, are key figures at the WMF along with Scott Lavender who has been a major player on the Welsh music scene for many years.

During February, the Mark Evans-directed film *Beautiful Mistake* was produced in Cardiff. It features an array of songs performed over a nine-day period in a studio setting by an assortment of Welsh musicians. John Cale (most famous for his days with the avant-garde rock group Velvet Underground) provides the central theme for the film. He contributes some excellent songs as well as film clips to add enlightening social and personal commentary. Catatonia feature twice in the film singing "Whispering Room" written by Owen and a John Cale composition entitled "Close Watch". Cerys appeared to be very relaxed during the production.

Equally Cursed and Blessed was released on Tuesday, March 28th with "Road Rage" and "Mulder and Scully" from *International Velvet* added for the US market. Atlantic Records then released "Road Rage" on April 20th as the first single on the label. Cerys may have had other ideas, especially as she was obviously trying to reduce the number of times they performed "Mulder and Scully".

The fact that Atlantic chose "Road Rage" showed greater sense than that displayed by their previous record company. It is strange to observe that Atlantic marketed Catatonia in the USA by directly promoting the band, while Warners/Vapor tried to force them on to local audiences with an approach more suited to selling medicines from the back of a covered wagon.

Cerys was in demand from the US media and did a cover shot and interview for the April issue of *Details*. Unfortunately, the American jinx on Catatonia struck again when on the eve of flying out to the USA, Aled was taken ill with appendicitis. He was left behind with a view to him joining the rest of the band a few days later, but he was hospitalized in the UK and thus the promotions were postponed.

This was what was reported at the time, but it was eventually revealed to be a cover up story. Cerys admitted later that she had been having problems bordering on a nervous breakdown for quite some time and this had been the reason behind canceling both the December 1999 arena tour and this one in the US.

"I cocked that up, didn't I?" she said.

Inevitably this led to further media speculation that the band were on the verge of splitting up. Cerys was struggling to get her enthusiasm and conviction back. The sheer volume of work had drained her spirit. "I could never stop singing but you don't want to work like an automaton do you?"

She then went to try and sort her problems out, "to the worst possible place for a while – Los Angeles" while the rest of the group were in New York.

Meanwhile the album failed to reach the *Billboard* top hundred. Whilst the critics were enthusiastic, it appeared that the US record buyers had other ideas. By their own admission, Catatonia were not seeking to storm America. Cerys had indicated that they would be happy just to slot in somewhere.

The paranoia that has infected the UK music industry, concerning making it big in America, has harmed and ruined many home grown acts and tested the patience of the UK fans who want new material and concerts from their favourites. In May, the Super Furry Animals put the US market beautifully into perspective before a scheduled North American tour. "They were not going out with the intention to conquer America, they were going to make love to it."

It became obvious that for Catatonia the next tilt at the USA would be much further down the road.

In June S4C held a charity auction in Carmarthen for the NSPCC. The band is still a highly respected outfit, especially in Wales, and has regularly tried to help various charities. The Welsh rugby shirt worn by Cerys at the opening ceremony fetched either £450 or £750 (according to which newspaper you read). Welsh actor Stifyn Parri took the shirt to Los Angeles in the autumn and gave it to Dylan Douglas, the baby son of Michael Douglas and Stifyn's friend Catherine Zeta Jones. Stifyn said, "What better present could there be?"

By this time Catatonia were beginning to work on their major objective for 2000, to write and record the next album. To this end they went to the lengths of retiring to a remote farm in Wales to write, rehearse and demo material, a process which spawned "loads of new songs". It was also rumoured that there was a possibility of more Matthews/Roberts songs as the band worked at their secret hideout during late spring and early summer. There was a slight break in the proceedings, when, across the Bristol Channel on June 24th, there was a surprise in store for many pop fans. The Pet Shop Boys were playing the Pyramid Stage at Glastonbury. During their set, Neil Tennant announced, "The next song was originally recorded by Dusty Springfield. Tonight we will do it with a very special friend of ours" – the crowd went wild as Cerys walked onto the stage. She has always admired Dusty Springfield and had planned to sing the duet a year earlier. Stunningly glamorous, she captivated the crowd before leaving to a rousing ovation.

Catatonia continued to work on preparations for the new album, but then tragedy struck. On Sunday 30th July, Barry Cawley, the band's guitar technician was killed whilst cycling near Bettws y Coed, North Wales. Like Paul and Mark, Barry came from Llanrwst. He was the best friend of Mark and a close friend of Cerys and the rest of the band.

Barry had been a member of Y Cyrff and worked with Catatonia since the early days. The band suspended work immediately. Mark undertook the responsibility of dealing with the media and informed the press that Cerys was devastated and had returned home to come to terms with her sorrow. This is typical of Mark. Barry's death was a savage blow to him. It shattered him personally but he tried to hide it in public.

Adam's Catatonia website received tributes from fans throughout the world. Some recalled personal meetings on tours, others offered condolences, but all of them mourned the loss. A couple of weeks before the tragedy, a young fan (Laura Derbyshire) had made Cerys some "Cursed and Blessed" bracelets and asked me if I could arrange to get them to her. While Cerys was grieving, she took time out to personally write a reply to the fan and thank her for the "gorgeous gesture". Laura was overjoyed. This is the Cerys that the fans know, and it is actions like this that endear the group to the fanbase.

The Welsh population had not forgotten about Catatonia during their self-imposed exile and Owen and Aled were asked to be judges in the pop music section at the Eisteddfod that was held at Llanelli between August 5th and 12th.

It was refreshing to see the entire band back in Wales again, although they did not socialise together very much. It was like old times and perhaps an omen for the future. Cerys was to be seen frequenting the Cardiff nightlife scene, including one hen party that started on a Saturday night and seemed to continue at assorted venues for the rest of the week.

Towards the end of August, the band moved into the Music Box Rehearsal Rooms in Cardiff for a week long session to practise songs for the new album that was given the working title "It's What's Not There, That Makes What's There What It Is."

While they were there, the *New Musical Express* interviewed Cerys. She admitted to the paper that she had almost quit the band in 1999 after a nervous breakdown.

"I had a bit of a breakdown and I had to stop. I think, um, yeah, possibly through overwork. I'd never thought beyond being a singer in the band and then suddenly, um, things get a bit beyond, you know? We've been touring solidly since '93, '94. We had a brilliant two years with the hit singles and that. But I'd never thought beyond that, and suddenly we were."

People are complex, highly individual and unique in personality. Our behaviour is affected by many factors in our lives and we are often unaware of the overall picture. Similarly, we are all unique in how we adjust to changes in our environment. The management author Hans Selye describes stress as "the rate of all the wear and tear caused by life." This appeared to sum up Cerys' situation since the success of "Mulder and Scully". Stress itself is inevitable and sometimes it can be beneficial, but unreasonable stress affects a person's ability and judgement.

When a band is working hard to break through to the heady heights of pop stardom, they are generally very close to each other, but when success arrives, relationships within the group often become more distant. This is not a criticism, it is a fact of life. Cerys is not a shrinking violet, and the boys are not publicity seekers. Few could blame her for milking success. I think most people would have done the same, but the band seemed to become less close as a unit than before.

Cerys had been contributing less of the songwriting and musical input to Catatonia, and perhaps unknowingly this had been part of the problem. Despite her being a fiercely independent person, she is also very homely and loves her family and friends, and I believe that whilst this rise to super-stardom gave her much pleasure, it eventually contributed to her physical and mental exhaustion.

She was quizzed about whether the breakdown was anything to do with drink or drugs, to which she countered, "I've never denied that I work hard and I play hard." But it was a lack of conviction and not enjoying what she was doing that was the serious problem. She would not be tied down to the exact point of the breakdown.

A mutual friend told me that according to Cerys, the interview did not quite convey what she was trying to explain. Personally, I don't think it was a nervous breakdown as such, rather a culmination of mental and nervous attrition. A breakdown would have ruled her out of foreign tours, duets, personal appearances etc, and this certainly did not happen. She had been pushed to breaking point and she needed to sort things out for herself. She has walked the cliff tops in Pembrokeshire often enough to know the right moment to step back.

Evidently, things had come to a head round about the time of the Netaid concert in October 1999 because the arena tour was cancelled shortly after. She really hit the bottle at that gig. The band put in a brilliant perfor-mance but towards the end of the concert proper she was really paralytic backstage. It reminded me all too well of how a certain arsehole had tried to cope with his problems in 1993.

Throughout 1999 there had been frequent instances where Cerys had become stressed out. In between these events she performed exceptionally well at gigs and seemed to enjoy life in flashes. The bad karma kept coming back and the culmination of all this seemingly drove her to the limit of her endurance. When you are the centre of attention, you can be the loneliest person in the world.

The pace of her life had been frenetic, especially as she is the original 24-carat party animal. It was no wonder she was exhausted. Everybody wanted a piece of Catatonia, everybody wanted a piece of Cerys.

She took on many solo ventures outside the group, some of which could have been therapeutic, others merely adding to her burden. There would also have been the Champagne Charlies telling her she had a better future going solo and promising her El Dorado, until their next star prospect came along.

Perhaps there was nobody to offer her support when it was needed. Nobody she could trust or confide in and help diffuse the pressure. There were plenty of celebrity arse-lickers telling her what they thought she wanted to hear, but we all need to be told how it is from time to time, even if we don't like it. It appears that few, if any, had been strong enough to tell her. Perhaps a Personal Manager/Advisor, disassociated from her management and record company, would have been the answer – it works for some. Other than that, a close friend with good business sense.

However, the band were always there. As fame came their way in 1998, Mark, Aled, Paul and Owen were content to let Cerys get the lioness's share of the adulation and she was happy to receive it. Their concern was that it might get too much for her. Eventually when the time came, Cerys explained, "So, I stopped. I'm grateful to the boys in my band for being patient with me and letting me go and wander around for a while."

She stayed in London and also visited the North of England. One of my friends thought he saw her at a Johnny Marr gig at Sheffield Leadmill, but he also thought Liam Gallagher was there, so the jury is out on that one. All of this allowed her to take a break from "the old songs and feelings."

Fortunately, getting out of the hamster's cage had worked. "It was good to take a step back and get back to wanting to sing again and not just feel as if you're repeating yourself. That's what really drove me crazy. Things are back on course now. We've got fresh music and attitudes and it's like starting again."

A couple of weeks after the interview, Catatonia started recording at Rockfield Studios. They recruited the services of Clive Langer and Alan Winstanley who had worked with bands that Catatonia admired such as Madness and Dexy's Midnight Runners. When completed it was anticipated that the album and single would be promoted by a tour of smaller venues, thus satisfying the increasing desire for fans in the UK to see the band perform gigs, rather than festivals.

Whilst Catatonia were recording at Rockfield, Radio 1 held its annual *One Live* event. The chosen city this year was Cardiff. Obviously they wanted some input from a high profile Welsh band to boost the week long extravaganza. However, most of the bands were in the process of recording albums. I was at the launch party at Clwb Ifor and Cerys had sent a card to Steve Lamacq on behalf of the band, wishing Radio 1 well for the event and explaining that due to their commitments the band could not participate directly.

After completing work at Rockfield, Catatonia took a couple of weeks off before spending six weeks in a London studio mixing and enhancing the album. Following this, the band undertook further mixing and fine-tuning back at Paul's studio in his Cardiff home.

Owen could now be forgiven for having sleepless nights. He had become the very proud father of a baby boy, Herbie.

Late in November, we were treated to another example of the quirkiness of Cerys' nature. Madonna played a gig at the Brixton Academy on the 28th November. Long before the gig took place, Cerys had made it clear that she wanted to attend. This seemed very strange because Cerys had not been very complementary about Madonna in earlier interviews, saying things like, "I'm fed up with her, she's so boring. She's just lost it." On another occasion, "I'm not a fan of Madonna. I think she functions in binary numbers." Perhaps Cerys' reasoning was that this was a celebs' night out and that this would remind the pop world that she was very much alive and kicking.

The following evening saw the premiere of the film *Beautiful Mistake* at the 12th International Film Festival of Wales held in Cardiff. James Dean Bradfield from the Manic Street Preachers and Cerys were expected to be the leading celebrities that night. Unfortunately, Cerys did not attend, which came as a surprise and disappointment to the fans that turned up. Evidently, all was still not completely well in her life, and the band was represented by Paul instead.

The media were warming to the reappearance of Catatonia and *Melody Maker* featured Cerys on its centre pages of the December 13th issue. Sadly, the news then broke that due to plummeting sales this long-established magazine would cease publication with its Christmas edition and would be absorbed by the *NME*.

It was hoped that the album would be completed by early December but this target was not met. Further work was required and the band spent a week in the studio in the middle of January 2001 and were still working on it in February when Cerys contacted *NME.com*. She explained that the album (still referred to by its working title of "It's What's Not There, That Makes What's There, What It Is") was "darker and more macabre than its predecessors". Mark had contributed most of the lyrics and "they are pretty astonishing".

Tracks included "Long Time Lonely", "Misogyny", "Village Idiots" and "Stone By Stone" which was tipped to be the first single released from the album.

A source close to the band revealed on the internet that the record company had not been too impressed with some of the vocal mixes, hence the additional studio time. The band was also very keen to get everything right which is probably another contributory factor to its delay.

In February, there was good news for the band's fans when it was announced that Catatonia would headline a concert to publicise the Campaign for a Minimum Wage. to be held at the Manchester Evening News Arena on 28th April, with Toploader, Idlewild, Wheatas and the Dumdums.

But what of Cerys? Would she be up for it? The question was answered on March 3rd on a BBC2 programme *The Life and Lyrics of Kirsty McColl.* Supported by Jools Holland, Cerys brilliantly sang "Fifteen Minutes". The message was very clear – I am back and Catatonia are going to take everybody by storm.

Throughout their career, Catatonia have proved their great powers of endurance. Having had the best part of a year off, Cerys said she was beginning to feel better. Now the Millennium is out of the way it will be as good a time as ever for them to "start again".

In view of their exceptional ability and undoubted untapped potential, they are still under-achieving. They have within themselves the capability to be top of the heap. In this business though, those around you must match your ability and ensure that the potential is fully realised.

The answer is out there, at the end of the rainbow.

I DON'T KNOW WHERE IT IS I'M GOING

Take it from where you want to grow, there's always tomorrow.

Matthews/Roberts.

What does the future hold for Catatonia? They themselves have made references to bands having shelf lives. There are notable exceptions to this tenet such as the Rolling Stones. One major advantage Catatonia have is the composition of their fanbase. They have loyal supporters from all walks of life and all ages. They are also very popular outside the UK so the immediate prospects are encouraging. Increasing demands have been made on Cerys to work outside Catatonia, but this has happened to other bands and provided projects are managed sensibly then a dual career should be successful.

Cerys was once asked by *Select* magazine, "Have you ever wanted to go solo?" She responded, "I think everybody in any band ever has contemplated going their own way, but I have no reason to think about it. Why should I go solo when I have the best musicians and the best songwriters in the world by my side to argue with. Politically, emotionally and practically we hate each other, but, on the musical level, somehow it works. I would be a right twat if I left."

Whatever the future has in store for her, she would do well to learn from her past. Cerys has a tremendous yet fragile talent. When she is up for it, she is the finest female pop singer in the UK. Indeed, the world could be her oyster. She has the ability and potential to be ranked as "one of the truly great singers", yet in this field she is only in her infancy. The only person standing in the way of her achieving this accolade, either with Catatonia or as a solo artist, is Cerys Matthews herself. Clearly, Cerys must at times be a pain to manage, but to maximise her potential, she needs management strong enough to guide her. She has her own opinions, but the last thing she needs is to be surrounded with "yes men" organising her.

Catatonia would rather be recording or playing live than getting bogged down with promotional chores, even though this sort of work usually falls on Cerys. Hopefully, all parties will have learned from the problems that she has encountered, because there is no guarantee that there won't be a repeat. She has a very strong personality, but so had Judy Garland and others since. The walls of many entertainment executives' offices are covered with photographs of stars whose lights have been extinguished by the pressures of overload.

Of course everybody wants to interview Cerys, but this is where management and record companies have to be selective. She is their investment. Is it better to go for a quickfire, huge profit and to hell with it if she suffers, or is it preferable to go for a regular steady earner and spread the promotional duties wider? Someone has to be prepared to tell promoters that Catatonia is a band and that duties are shared. I can't help but recall what Mark said about playing the same places too regularly, too often. Over exposing a star has the same effect.

When being interviewed Cerys has caused eyebrows to be raised by admitting that she always knew she was a good singer and was not surprised about the band's achievements. I never doubted both claims, but she seemed to have difficulty in adjusting to dealing with the constant pressures on her life that her singing and media magnetism had generated.

Cerys has admitted to having a "nervous breakdown" and needed time out to sort herself out. Having been in a similar situation myself, I can appreciate that this is neither a short or easy journey to make.

Many people speak highly of her and are amazed how she comes across as a "nice, friendly, ordinary person. Nothing like a pop star." She confesses to becoming a fidget if she has nothing to occupy her attention, and perhaps some active involvement in other areas, not necessarily related to music, could provide the key to maintaining her enthusiasm.

At the time of writing, the band has released three albums. I seem to be in a minority because I do not have a favourite one. Whatever mood I am in usually dictates which album goes on my CD player. One sign of a talented band is the ability to vary the content and style of each album so that it reflects where they were at that particular time. When that same band can easily play selections from all of its albums at live gigs to the satisfaction of fans old and new, then you have a winning formula. To date that is the achievement of Catatonia. I see no reason why that should not continue.

Cerys is realistic about success but she does have ambitions. She never wants to give up singing, even to the point of threatening to jump off the Severn Bridge when the fortunes of Catatonia wane. "If I can't sing and have people enjoy it, I'm fucked." The desire will always be there and it should not be difficult to keep the enthusiasm up if handled sensibly.

In later life, one dream she has is to combine her singing and domestic talents. Hosting a TV programme – "Gardening With Cerys" combining pop singing, gardening and being a TV chef, with a bit of interior decorating thrown in.

It has been suggested that one area where Cerys could work away from the band successfully is acting. Rhys Ifans, director of *Twin Town,* the "Mulder and Scully" video and friend of the band thinks, "Cerys Matthews would be a fantastic actress. It's a question of charisma and the ability to focus it, and Cerys is the embodiment of both. You can tell by her lyrics that she would be a good actress because she's got a real understanding of the human condition. And if you've got an understanding of words then you're halfway to being a good actor."

Cerys, however, is not convinced and claims not to be interested in acting. In interviews she has identified other ventures that she would be interested in – a karaoke and a Sushi bar take her fancy. She has even thought of a name for her Sushi bar – "Can You Smell My Fish?" Most of her ideas, not surprisingly, are associated with things that are of personal interest to her.

Should the Catatonia bandwagon stop rolling one day, what would the boys do? Mark has proved he is one of the most gifted songwiters around at the moment so that could be one calling. I doubt he will be pursuing a career on the keyboards, but if his footballing days are numbered he could always get a game with Sheffield Wednesday. Owen, over the past couple of years, has also written some captivating material. I suppose the burning question would be – could the same quality of songs be produced for an unknown singer, or without the group brain-storming sessions in the studio? The same would apply to Cerys. She has proved both on record and through karaoke that she can sing cover versions, but it is the Catatonia songs that the public love and associate with her. This has to be a well that she must surely draw from.

Paul, meanwhile, has demonstrated his abilities in track mixing and production, whilst perhaps Aled has his eyes set on opening a catering establishment, as he once told *New Musical Express* that he worries about old people demanding specific pieces of fish in the chip shop. "As far as I'm concerned you take what you're given and shut the fuck up." That would be my kind of place.

So, what does the future hold for me?

Friends of mine have commented that I have had a tough life. I disagree. It is all relative. I had a series of devastating events happen to me in a short space of time. Before then, and subsequently afterwards, I have taken and enjoyed each day as it comes. I can look at the news programmes on TV every day and see children all over the world suffering. Their best day will never be as good as my worst. It makes me ashamed to think of how I let my problems get me down. But if I had my life over again, I know I would react exactly the same way and hopefully there would be another Catatonia to throw me a lifeline via their music.

Just like Mark and Owen, my schoolteachers too made predictions about me. My English teacher thought that I would one day write a worthwhile book. My music teacher was less complementary. He considered that music and myself were total strangers and every effort should be made to keep us apart. His name was Huw Parry, and he was Welsh.

Sitting in a cold and dark Valleys Chapel, with rain dripping through a leaky roof onto my head on a wintry November night would have been paradise compared to how he presented music to us. To prove him wrong, I was determined to discover outside of the classroom, just what pleasure music can offer.

So, probably for all the wrong reasons, it was the result of an old Welshman's opinion that instilled into me a love of music. Then, when I had lost all grasp of the reality of life, it was to be a band of young Welsh people who rekindled the passion within me.

As long as Catatonia play, I will support them. We have both come a long way over the past few years. They have achieved the rewards that they deserve, although on many occasions it seemed it was not going to be the case. I am still no wiser as to what it was that grabbed my attention on that fateful night – some mysteries are perhaps best left unsolved. If it had not been for that one-way bonding, the catalyst that sparked of my battle for survival, then I would not have made it.

Wales needs no recommendation from me. I have fallen in love with its beauty as I have travelled round, engrossed in watching bands, and as a tourist.

The people of Wales greatly assisted me when I most needed support and since I have recovered and became my old self, they have befriended me more so. I have had some good nights drinking with the men, and I have never encountered so many beautiful ladies as there are in the Principality. Having accounted for two passions, now comes the third. I have achieved my main aim and have become involved with the development of new bands.

On matters Catatonia, chivalry dictates that I should allow "The Lady" the last word. Cerys was asked the following question by *Welsh Bands Weekly*.

Apart from your music, what do you want to be best known for?

"Can I be really soppy," she replied, "and say being a good friend to people? I love my friends and I know a lot of good people. And I'd like to be remembered as always being willing to try everything once."

Diolch yn fawr.

EPILOGUE

When I saw Judy sing, I did not know that it would be for the last time, and that shortly she would be dead. Nearly 200 miles away, there was a baby girl keeping her first audience happy. This infant, sometime in the future would be a part of a band that saved my life... I could not possibly foresee either event, but I am greatly privileged to have seen both ladies. Perfection never makes a dream – that is why you remember it.

The Author.

As I mentioned earlier, the tone of the July 8th interview with *The Daily Telegraph* prompted me to write the epilogue before I commenced the book. Only a biography about Catatonia could start from the back page. The subsequent events with the tabloid press and other media have only added to the sentiments. Strong-willed people succumb to being overloaded with work, and from being hounded by the press far more frequently than those of a less resilient character. Is it necessary to try and tarnish a gilded lily for the price of thirty pieces of silver in the till? Stars need their rest, their space and their public and personal dignity.

There was once a lady with a very precocious talent. She had been described as, "An angel with spurs." Her public life became the property of her management and as her career developed, she was overcome with the pace of her success. Her management ensured there was always a supply of booze and drugs available as this helped keep her public image intact.

When she was down, she would drink whatever was to hand and then she said, "I put on my lipstick, see my stockings are straight and go out there and sing." She was described as:

"A singer whose way with a song is nothing short of marvellous."

"A star, the genuine, outsize article."

"Superb as ever, enchantingly vulnerable."

I consider myself very, very fortunate to have seen one of her final performances in cabaret, in London, shortly before the final overdose took her from us. Her management had destroyed her life with the punishing work schedule they organised for her in the early stages of her fame. The industry she had graced so magnificently caused her early death.

The double irony is that London finally sucked the life out of this lady, coincidentally, in 1969.

The singer I had seen was still a star at the time, and to many she always will be, especially to a little lady who was then only three months old. It was not Little Dorothy I had seen, for sadly, she had long since gone, but it was the legendary Judy Garland.

If only this hamster had been allowed out of the wheel occasionally, she may have graced us with her presence for longer. Whilst the death of a star, whether physically or metaphorically, is upsetting to many for a short time, the star is quickly replaced. What can never be replaced is the person who was the star – the beautiful, warm person who, away from the limelight is just flesh and blood and some mother's child.

Cerys loves the films and music of Judy Garland and so I will conclude with some words spoken by Dorothy in *The Wizard Of Oz* which to me seem more than appropriate sentiments for "The Lady" from Wales.

"If I ever go looking for my heart's desire again, I won't look any further than my own backyard, because if it isn't there, I never really lost it to begin with."

CATATONIA DISCOGRAPHY

SINGLES and EPs

1993
FOR TINKERBELL EP
Release: September Label Crai CraiCD039L (CD), Crai CO39B (Tape)

1994
HOOKED
Release: May. Label Crai CraiCD042B (CD)
WHALE
Release: August. Label Rough Trade Singles 7" Viinyl

1995
BLEED
Release: February. Label Nursery NYSCD12/NYS12L (CD), 7" Vinyl (1,000 copies)
CHRISTMAS '95
Released in December free to members on Catatonia's mailing list. 7" Vinyl (1,000 copies)

1996
SWEET CATATONIA
Release: January 18. Label Blanco Y Negro NEG85CD (CD). NEG85CAS (Cassette). NEG85X (7" Vinyl)
LOST CAT
Release: April. Label Blanco Y Negro NEG88CD1 (CD 1). NEG88CD2 (CD 2).NEG88CAS (Cassette). NEG88X (7" Vinyl)
YOU'VE GOT A LOT TO ANSWER FOR
Release: August 26. Label Blanco Y Negro NEG93CD1 (CD 1). NEG93CD2 (CD 2). NEG93CAS (Cassette) NEG93 (7" Vinyl)
BLEED
Release: November 18. Label Blanco Y Negro NEG97CD1 (CD 1). NEG97CD2 (CD 2). NEG97 CASS (Cassette). NEG97 (7" Vinyl)

SINGLES and EPs (continued)

1997
I AM THE MOB
Release: September 29. Label Blanco Y Negro NEG107CD (CD). NEG107CASS
(Cassette). NEG107 (7" Vinyl)

1998
MULDER AND SCULLY
Release: January 19. Label Blanco Y Negro NEG109CD (CD).
NEG109CASS(Cassette). NEG109 (7" Vinyl)
ROAD RAGE
Release: April 20. Label Blanco Y Negro NEG112CD (CD). NEG112CASS(Cassette).
NEG112 (7" Vinyl)
STRANGE GLUE
Release: July 20. Label Blanco Y Negro NEG113CD (CD). NEG113C (Cassette).
NEG113 (7"Vinyl)
GAME ON
Release: October 26. Label Blanco Y Negro NEG114CD (CD). NEG 114C (Cassette)
NEG 114 (7" Vinyl)

1999
DEAD FROM THE WAIST DOWN
Release: March 29. Label Blanco Y Negro NEG115CD (CD). NEG115C (Cassette).
NEG115 (7" Vinyl)
LONDINIUM
Release: July 12. Label Blanco Y Negro NEG117CD (CD). NEG117C (Cassette).
NEG117 (7" Vinyl)
KARAOKE QUEEN
Release: November 1. Label Blanco Y Negro NEG119CD (CD). NEG119C (Cassette).
NEG119 (7" Vinyl)

ALBUMS

1995
THE SUBLIME MAGIC OF...
Release: November. Japanese import. Label Nursery NYSCD12X (CD)

1996
TOURIST
Release: July. Japanese Import. WPCR-769
WAY BEYOND BLUE
Release: September 30. Label Blanco Y Negro 0630163052 (CD). 0630163054
(Cassette). 0630163051 (LP)

ALBUMS (continued)

1998
INTERNATIONAL VELVET
Release: February 2. Label Blanco Y Negro 3984208340 (CD). 3984208342
(Cassette). 3984208341 (LP)
CATATONIA 1993/1994
Release: December 14. Label CRAI CD064 (CD).

1999
EQUALLY CURSED AND BLESSED
Release: April 12. Label Blanco Y Negro 3984270942 (CD). 3984270941 (LP)

COMPILATIONS

Catatonia song (s) in italics
1993
Ap ELVIS
Release: April 8. Label Ankst Ankst 038. *Gyda Gwen*
POP PETHDAU
Release: December. Label Ankst Video Compilation Ankst 048. *Difrycheulyd
Dimbran*

1994
VOLUME 12
Release: May. 12VCD12. *Dream On*

1995
S4C MAKES ME WANT TO SMOKE CRACK (VOL 1)
Release: February. Label Ankst Records Atol 2. *Cariadon Ffol*
TRISKADEKAPHILIA
Release: December. Label Ankst Records Ankst CD061 (CD). Ankst061C (Cassette).
Gwe. Iago M

1996
THE PHOENIX ALBUM
CD of bands who played the Festival. *Way Beyond Blue*
DIAL M FOR MERTHYR
Label Fierce Panda / Townhill Records. NONGCD02 (CD). NONGLP02 (Double LP).
To And Fro
VOLUME 17
Release: December. 17VCD17. *Mickey (aka Some Half Baked Ideal Called
Wonderful)*

ALBUMS (continued)

1997
TWIN TOWN
Release:April 11th. Label Polygram 540 718-2. *You've Got A Lot To Answer For*
SPLASH
Release: July. Q Magazine compilation with Q130. *You've Got A Lot To Answer For*

COLLABORATIONS

1998
THE BALLAD OF TOM JONES
Release: March 23. SPACE featuring CERYS CDGUT18 (CD). GUT18 (Cassette)

1999
BABY IT'S COLD OUTSIDE
Release: December 6. TOM JONES and CERYS from CATATONIA. CDGUT29 (CD 1
& 2). GUT29 (Cassette)

ACKNOWLEDGEMENTS AND SOURCES

Adam's Catatonia Website, *Bassist* Magazine, *Buzz*, *Daily Telegraph*, *Loaded*, *Melody Maker*, *New Musical Express*, *Q* magazine, *Raygun* magazine, *Roadster* magazine, *Select*, *Sky* magazine, *Wales On Sunday*, *Welsh Bands Weekly*, John Parry, Paul Gorman, Alice At MoonBeats, Marc Casnewydd and Strawberry, Owain at Ankst, Ceri Morgan, David and Jeni Wright.

SAF and Firefly Titles

All SAF and Firefly titles are available by mail order from the world famous Helter Skelter bookshop.

You can either phone or fax your order to Helter Skelter on the following numbers:

Telephone: +44 (0)20 7836 1151 or Fax: +44 (0)20 7240 9880
Office hours: Mon-Fri 10:00am - 7:00pm,
Sat: 10:00am - 6:00pm, Sun: closed.

Postage prices per book worldwide are as follows:

UK & Channel Islands	£1.50
Europe & Eire (air)	£2.95
USA, Canada (air)	£7.50
Australasia, Far East (air)	£9.00
Overseas (surface)	£2.50

You can also write enclosing a cheque, International Money Order, or registered cash. Please include postage. DO NOT send cash. DO NOT send foreign currency, or cheques drawn on an overseas bank. Send to:

Helter Skelter Bookshop,
4 Denmark Street, London, WC2H 8LL, United Kingdom.
If you are in London come and visit us, and browse the titles in person!!

Email: helter@skelter.demon.co.uk
Website: http://www.skelter.demon.co.uk

For the latest on SAF and Firefly titles check the SAF website:

www.safpublishing.com